Prayer
without
Ceasing

Prayer without Ceasing

Breath Prayers

by Kathleen S. Lewis

Prescott Press

Prescott Press
P.O. Box 53788
Lafayette, Louisiana 70505

Cover photo copyright © 1996,
Comstock, Inc.

Library of Congress Card Catalog
Number 97-69269
ISBN 0-933451-37-7

Printed in the U.S.A.

Contents

Introduction

It's a privilege and honor to be able to share with you how the Lord is teaching me to pray without ceasing, using breath prayer as I journey through life on my way home to heaven. I don't want the focus to be on the events and circumstances of my life, but on what God is doing through those events and circumstances.

The Lord is taking the wonderful and awful, the best and worst, the good and bad, and is redeeming and blessing it all in His perfect wisdom, grace, and timing in each moment of each day! Even as I write and you read, His redemptive process is at work.

I have no illusions about what I have to say as being important, wonderful, or grand. The only thing important, wonderful, or grand that may occur, is where what I might have to share connects with where you are, have been, and are going in your life. If the Holy Spirit can use any one thing to touch and carry you one step farther on your journey, a miracle and victory has occurred.

I am just beginning to realize the power of what I am going to write about. Read with caution. Breath prayers may change your life forever. They have been and are changing my life, breath by breath.

I fear I may be totally inadequate to put into words what has and is happening. I can only trust it's not what I share that's important, but how the Holy Spirit might use it in your life. My only mandate is to share as honestly as I know how. I feel as if I am treading on holy ground.

I stand in joy, awe, and wonder, as I watch other people catch on to breath prayers, and use them in their lives. I have experienced and witnessed transformation and transcendence of circumstances occurring in my life, and in the lives of those who embrace and use breath prayers.

Life, by itself, without any problems is a daily struggle. When you add in complications such as divorce, illness, financial problems, relationship tangles, etc., life can become a raging battle. You need all of the victory skills possible to keep your lifeship balanced, afloat, and moving.

All too often, you can make your pain and trouble your main focus. Obsessional, anxious thinking takes over your brain. Pain, fatigue, confusion, doubt, fear, anger, bitterness, and depression can create a vicious, tyrannical thought cycle and become your god instead of a guide, as they were meant to be. Whatever becomes your main focus displaces God.

As a child of God, nurse, medical psychotherapist, writer, speaker, person with SLE (systemic lupus erythematosus), divorcee, single parent, recovering codependent, I have helped others on the battlefield of daily living. I try to teach people the victory skill I have found in using breath prayers in the middle of many life crises.

Breath prayers have helped me survive moment by moment to make it one more step, day, task, feeling, and challenge at a time to take me further into my tomorrows. I find myself not just surviving but transcending and soaring! Praying on the breath is not just a coping skill, but a victory skill.

One of the greatest weapons I have found to wage against the campaigns of daily living is breath prayers. It is very simply, the claiming of a Scripture as I breathe out, over and over. The average person breathes approximately 16 times a minute, 960 times an hour, and 23,040 a day. What an opportunity to pray the Scripture.

The breath prayer is enhanced by saying it when falling asleep, waking up, and during periods of deep meditation, when the subconscious mind is more accessible to the conscious mind. Meditating is mentioned throughout the Bible, especially in the Psalms. Western religion has excluded meditation, which is very scripturally based.

In Eastern areas where the Lord lived, there is emphasis on "being." The Western world and religion seem to promote becoming a "human doing" rather than a "human being." This is a "how to" book that tells you how to change from the inside out, instead of from the outside in.

In the following pages, I'll tell in devotional form of my journey in learning to breathe scriptural affirmations, as a prayer on the exhaling of my breath. The devotionals will feature a Scripture, followed by the breath prayer, and then some comments. There'll be a chapter on how to create your own breath prayers, appendices on the theory of why breath prayers work, and a listing of breath prayers by topic.

Breath prayers will open you up to the words and thoughts of the Great "I Am" and your own being. The end results will hopefully be your doing and will become an overflow of your being, not the reverse. You'll find memorization of Scripture take on a whole different impetus, and take off like a rocket.

Some breath prayers may leap off the pages and right into your life. Others may not. The breath prayer that "fits" you at the time can be almost diagnostic, as to where you are at the moment. There will be an "AHA!" experience when you find the breath prayer that suits where you are.

Breath prayers are a means of fulfilling the admonition in God's Word: Thessalonians 5:16, "Pray without ceasing;" in Philippians 4:8, "Think on these things;" Joshua 1:8, "You shall meditate in the Book day and night;" and in Ephesians 6:17, "Take the sword of the Spirit, which is the word of God!"

Your thoughts are the gateway to your being. Most of your thoughts are in the unconscious mind, 90 percent of your mind. Every thought you have registers with changes in the hormones, chemicals, muscles, breathing, and immune system in your body. Breath prayers can keep your thoughts focused on the Scripture and even access your unconscious thoughts!

Hebrews 4:12 describes the power of the Scripture: "For the word of God is living and powerful, and sharper than any two-edged sword, piercing even to the division of soul and spirit, and of joints and marrow, and is a discerner of thoughts and intents of the heart." What mighty power there is in using that Scripture, which is the sword of the Spirit, as a means to pray on each exhalation.

With breath prayers you take the sword of the Word, pray it on your breath, and give it to the Holy Spirit. Your body is the temple of the Holy Spirit. By claiming a breath prayer as you exhale, you are wrapping your body and mind, the temple of the Holy Spirit, around the sword of the Holy Spirit, the Scripture. Wow!

Read carefully! This is forceful stuff! Communing with God by opening myself to the power of the Holy Spirit's sword through breath prayers is taking me places in my life I could never have imagined, or otherwise dreamed. The impossible is becoming possible.

The Lord turns crises into celebration, brokenness into blessedness, wounds into the wonderful, victims into victors, trouble into triumph, and trash into treasure! He redeems all things in His perfect wisdom, grace, and timing. Praise the Lord!

Chapter One

The How To's

The first step in using breath prayers is to learn to catch yourself stepping on the stress spiral escalator. Use your thoughts and body's corresponding sensations to those thoughts, as your clues, cues, and guides. Emotions are where the thoughts of your mind and body manifestations (i.e., headache, stomach upset, muscle tension, etc.) marry. Your thoughts can jerk your body around. Your body can trigger your thoughts. Each can propel the other.

Become aware of where and how your body uniquely manifests stress for you. Then back up to identify what you're thinking. Your thoughts may manifest in your body . . . your head, neck, back, throat, chest, stomach, or any other area. You need to observe and become familiar with a behavior pattern before you can change it.

Not processing, inhibiting, repressing, or suppressing your anxious thoughts can cause physical and emotional stress, "dis-ease," and imbalance. The functioning of your immune system, the action of your heart and vascular system, and the biochemical working of your brain, nervous, and hormonal system are affected by your thoughts.

One way of examining and letting your thoughts go is to journal them. Journaling is a means of harnessing the drunken monkey of your mind. All this monkey does is lead you into useless, nonproductive, rambling, circular, obsessive thoughts. You can't think straight.

Journaling helps you process and harness your thoughts and feelings in a meaningful way. Turning thoughts into language, spoken or written, alter the way they are represented and understood in your mind. Once an experience is put into language, you can better understand it and put it behind you.

I journal in the form of a prayer. Prayer is a form of confiding, or disclosure. Putting a prayer into written form makes it even more powerful and useful by harnessing your prayer thoughts. It has been shown that disclosure in written form, even with no expectation of anyone reading it, reduces stress. Prayer journaling involves a body/mind/spirit workout. Your thoughts are opened to the Holy Spirit and can be extremely powerful.

I prayer journal my feelings and thoughts in a conversation with God on a daily basis. This helps me see and identify where my thoughts are leading me. With prayer journaling, I recognize and challenge unhealthy thinking. Then I can channel my thoughts in a healthier, productive direction. Healthy thinking includes, both negative and positive thoughts.

My thoughts and resulting feelings, are spread on a blank page before the Holy Spirit. Asking for counsel, comfort, instruction, healing, guidance, direction, understanding, insight, wisdom, protection, and blessing, invokes the leading of the Holy Spirit when my heart, mind, and spirit are too overloaded to even know what to pray.

I have walked through situations that were loaded with hidden land mines. With the leading of the Holy Spirit by using breath prayers, I have not only miraculously walked right through, but actually transcended thorny circumstances and avoided being blown out of the water without even knowing it. It is only in looking back that I realize the miracle, victory, blessing, and redemption.

Emotions (thoughts and their corresponding body manifestations) can be a beautiful healing energy, force, and guide. You keep yourself healthy only if you listen to, experience, make sense of, and process your emotions in every way possible. Only then can you release the flow of your emotions and be set free to move on in your life. You putrefy and stink when you try to dam up your emotions.

You can use counseling, physical exercise, crying out, moaning, groaning, journaling, music, singing, creative/stereophonic/aerobic crying, and many other routes to harness and process the emotions stirred by your mind and body. Your emotions can become navigational guides, to carry you down the river of your life. You make them your guide, not your god or main focus.

It can be very helpful to cry hard with gut-wrenching force. Polite sniffling just doesn't get the job done. Letting the tears flow, while moaning, groaning, or yelling processes and releases emotions.

Tears are like the safety valve on a pressure cooker, which blows out when the pressure builds to a dangerous level. I've blown a safety valve from a pressure cooker into the ceiling before. Boy, was I glad for it!

Tears

Tears can release the pain,
Wash away the strain
Caused by your hurt and grief
Bringing joy, peace, and release.

Tears can tap into strength
You never knew you had before
To keep you from going to the
brink
Your confidence and faith re-
store.

With grief, anger, and tears let
go
Dance and laughter can flow
From your full and overflowing
cup
That you never thought to fill
up.

Held inside with the tears
Were your anger, guilt, and
fears . . .
The good things were also
trapped
Just waiting to be unwrapped.

With all the bad things released
You can then find rest and
peace.

Let the tears run and freely flow
Or other good things you'll
never know.

Shutting down on, denying, repressing, or suppressing emotions
without processing them through your
mind, body, and spirit is like trying
to sit on a volcano that is about to
erupt. Asking your body to hold on
to the energy of emotions residing in
your mind and body creates a muscle
tension, fatigue, stress, imbalance, and
ultimately illness.

In January 1986 I had a hysterec-
tomy. The legal process of divorce was
in its final stages. January 29, three
days after I got home, was our 22nd
wedding anniversary. I was faced with
the decision of whether to hold in my
emotions, or cry and let it rip through
me.

Not crying would have stirred up
my SLE, causing me to feel sick. Creative, stereophonic, aerobic crying
while beating up on a pillow would
make my incision hurt. I chose to let
the pain and sorrow rip, pour, and
process through me. The next morn-

ing I woke up sore but not sick. I had been able to release those emotions by fully experiencing them.

You are set free to use your emotions in a healthy way as a guide, after releasing their physical energy and force. You can then sit down, prayer journal, look at your thoughts, and find an appropriate breath prayer to focus and center you on the Lord's promises.

Psychoneuroimmunology is a hot field right now. But, it doesn't consider the effects of the spirit on the whole picture of health. Health and wholeness are a balance between and within your mind, body, and spirit. If your body is struggling, a stress and pull is created on your spirit and mind.

If your mind is struggling, a strain and pull is created on your spirit and body. If your spirit is struggling, both your mind and body are put in a strain. Breath prayers spiritually break the mind/body feedback. Pull your mind off your body to do its own programmed healing and work.

One breath prayer doesn't fit all situations or people. The affirmation for the breath prayer is like a hand-and-glove fit for the circumstances of the moment. The affirmation needs to fit the space, time, experience, circumstance, people, and situation where you are in your life.

There will be an actual recognition reflex of your mind, body, and spirit when you find the right breath prayer. There will be an "AHA" and release on a cellular level, when you find and fix on the right breath prayer.

Finding the right breath prayer is a matter of trial and error. It takes practice using many breath prayers in different circumstances. What works for me may not work for another person. What works in one instance or situation may not work in another. The prayer truly needs to be the expression of the need of the breath of the moment.

It may take you awhile to find the right breath prayer for you at a particular time in the situation where you find yourself. Try a variety of affirmations. Pay attention to your mind/body/spirit response. You'll sense when a breath prayer just doesn't fit.

You will feel or sense the release, peace, and joy that the right breath prayer will bring. You'll know immediately when you've found the right breath prayer. There'll be an immediate centering, focusing, release, and energy flow.

Sometimes you'll be surprised at what the right breath prayer might be. The breath prayer that fits is usually diagnostic. The right breath prayer will reveal dramatically what the core "dis-ease" is. You might think that you need one thing, when you need an absolutely different thing.

Say the breath prayer with the perfectly balanced breath. The perfect breath is a 1 to 2 ratio for inhalation to exhalation. Inhale through your nose to a count of three. Exhale through your mouth to the count of six. Say your breath prayer to yourself as you exhale.

The affirmation needs to be in about seven syllables to fit with the exhaling of your breath. Seven syllables, give or take two or three syllables, is short enough to be easy to remember. Make it long enough to get in a complete thought in the time it takes to exhale.

Use the same pattern of breathing and repetition of the breath prayer while meditating. Meditating 20 to 30 minutes or longer a day uses the breath prayers you breathe throughout the day to empower the whole process, taking it to another level.

Using psychoacoustical or self-hypnosis tapes during your meditation time accesses the unconscious mind as you meditate, and gives an even greater boost. As long as you are thinking, your body can't relax. Meditating using breath prayers knocks your mind out of gear, allows your body to relax, lets your spirit loose, and can let in the Holy Spirit.

Imagine people, issues, or situations in your life and focus on the corresponding body sensations, while meditating and using the breath prayer that fits. As you lift your "dis-ease" to the Lord while claiming His promises, you'll find: vision and new understandings; release from the battle and struggle; healing and "wholing;" and balance of your mind, body, and spirit.

Praying without ceasing using breath prayers is not for God. It is for you. "I will keep him in perfect peace whose mind is stayed on me" (Isaiah 26:3). Using breath prayers will focus, balance, and center you in God's words, instead of fragmenting and scattering as you focus on the events and people around you.

Tightrope walkers don't look down at the wire. They pick a point ahead of them to focus on, as they carefully make their way across the wire. Looking down would be distracting and cause them to loose their balance and fall.

Walking on the Water

Though the storms of life rage
and toss about
The Lord is there with His hand
stretched out,
Saying, "Come to me across the
waves
That swirl and echo in distant
caves.

Fix your gaze on my eyes,
Not looking at the sea or skies.
Keep your hand reaching out
to mine.
I'll give you strength divine.
Don't be afraid, if the wind
seems strong,
Or the distance to me seems too
long.
My grace alone is sufficient for
you,
For any task you must do.

If you stop and focus on the
storm,
Fears and doubts will be born.
They will tempt you to shift your
focus
Will shake your faith, test your
trust."

As Peter came to Jesus across
the foam,
He allowed his gaze and attention to roam.
He began to sink in the fury of
the sea.
"Lord, save me!" was his frantic
plea.

Jesus quickly stretched out his
hand,
Took hold and lifted Peter to
stand.
"Oh! You of little faith. Why did
you doubt?'
He softly asked as he lifted Peter out.

Do you sink in the storms of
life
When trouble filled amidst the
strife?
Do you shift your gaze from
Jesus' face
Letting fear grip you, your faith
replace?

Jesus will gently reach out and
take your hand
And lift you above the waves to
stand.
Once more able to walk on the
water

Of life's storms and resulting disorder.

The Martial Arts and the use of good body mechanics teach you how to be balanced over a broad base of support, so you won't be thrown off center by an attack. Using breath prayers will center and focus you on God's promises and allow you to maintain your equilibrium. You can handle the blows of life being balanced in the broad base of support of scriptural affirmations claimed as a breath prayer.

You will find your own ways and adaptations to breath prayers, as you make them your own. They become your individual experience of prayer without ceasing, as it applies to your life and circumstances. You will discover what does and doesn't work for you through trial and error. Your faith, growth, and walk with the Holy Spirit will jump by leaps and bounds!

Chapter Two

Weakness

And He said to me, "My grace is sufficient for you, for My strength is made perfect in weakness."
— 2 Corinthians 12:9 (NAS)

"IN MY WEAKNESS IS YOUR STRENGTH!"

Many times when people realize all that I have lived through and live with, they say, "Wow! You are so strong!" I explain that it's just the opposite of what they think. It's when I give up my strength and claim my weakness that the Lord's strength is manifested and perfected in my weakness.

When I am feeling sick, tired, pain, fatigued, confused, lost, fearful, anxious . . . weak, I claim each time I breathe out "In my weakness is Your strength." I focus my thoughts away from all of my difficulties, and focus on the Lord. As I focus on Him, the thoughts that feed those feelings fall into the background.

If I choose to focus on those thoughts, I only enhance the end product of those thoughts. I get into a mind/body feedback loop where my thoughts and body's reactions go nowhere but in nonproductive circles. Emotions are the marriage of thoughts and manifestations in the body. By claiming breath prayers, I break the mind/body feedback loop.

By claiming my weakness made perfect in God's strength, I find the impossible becoming possible. I also find protection in breathing this prayer. My weak spots are where Satan as well as the Holy Spirit can enter in. I seal over my weakest spots and bind Satan with God's strength. I find protection by claiming God's strength at my weakest points and thoughts on each breath.

God's strength can be manifested and made perfect in my illness, divorce, fears, confusion, brokenness, lostness, codependency . . . weakness! I have so much weakness! The Lord has more than enough strength to be perfected and manifested in my weakness! In fact, it's in my weakness, not my strength, where I will be most yielded to the Lord and His leading.

You are strong only when you accept yourself as a "human being" (not a "human doing") and your weaknesses where God can manifest His strength. The sky is the limit when you realize that it's in your humanness, weaknesses, and limits that He can do His most miraculous work! As long as you focus on your own strength and control, the Lord can't manifest and perfect His strength in you.

Chapter Three

Grace

And He said to me, "My grace is sufficient for you, for My strength is made perfect in weakness."
—2 Corinthians 12:9 (NAS)

"YOUR GRACE IS SUFFICIENT FOR ME!"

People wonder at how I've survived the upheaval and storms in my life. Sometimes, so do I. My response is "Only by the grace of God!" It certainly hasn't been anything that I've done or accomplished. God has provided His grace in the moment for whatever hurdle or challenge was there! As I seek His grace in each moment, He provides all that I need, step by step, task by task, challenge by challenge.

Paul was asking for his thorn in the flesh to be taken away. The Lord's response was, "My grace is sufficient for you"! You and I are the same way. We want, magically removed, that discomfort, grain of sand, difficult relationship, or anything that makes us stretch and grow. The Lord wants us to stay with it and let Him redeem it, in His perfect wisdom, grace, and timing.

When you follow the leading of the Holy Spirit in the smallest thing, believe God is engineering your circumstances. The limitless power of God's grace is behind it. You draw on His grace in the moment of crisis, turmoil, and confusion . . . the present or exact moment. When you are drawing on God's grace, you can be humiliated by the circumstances of your life and manifest nothing but His grace.

God doesn't ask you to do anything easy or natural. You are called to do the things that by His grace He has perfectly fitted you to do. God's grace in my illness, divorce, and dysfunctional family has made me perfectly fitted to be a medical psychotherapist. I can help people and their families choose life and the challenges of living!

Nothing you can do will grant God's grace. It's a gift given freely and abundantly. Your job is only to be open to His grace. It is sufficient and all you need for any challenge or hurdle you face. It is enough to help you embrace and be all you are, no matter what you are facing.

Chapter Four

Hope and Confidence

"For Thou art my hope; O Lord God, Thou art my confidence from my youth"
—Psalms 71:5 (NAS)

"YOU ARE MY HOPE AND CONFIDENCE"

As my whole life has shattered and fallen apart around me, I have found over and over that only the Lord can be my hope and confidence. I've lost my health, ability to be substantially and gainfully employed, my profession, my marriage, support community as I knew it, right to apply for health or life insurance on my own, and just about everything in life as I knew it or dreamed it would be.

You can't make anything of this earth your hope and confidence, not any person, institution, health, possession, looks, intelligence, dreams, fantasies, support community, abilities, or so on. Everything on this plane is in constant motion and change. The only thing you can count on, is that you can't count on anything or anyone, except the Lord!

To stay healthy, you need to stay in motion physically, emotionally, and spiritually. When you get stuck, you get backed up, constipated, and become unhealthy. To be able to stay in motion, you need to learn how to let go of: children who grow up, move away, and on in their lives; dear ones who die; spouses who leave us; old expectation about life, ourselves, and former employees.

To be able to let go, you need to be able to relax. Just to be able to urinate, have a bowel movement, give birth, laugh, or cry, you need to let go! To grow, you need to be able to let go of the old, to move on to the new. When you try to hold on to things and keep them as they are, you block the flow of life in you with its unending surprises!

To relax, let go, and go with the flow of life, you need to make the Lord your only hope and confidence. I find myself clutching over and over when some difficulty comes my way. Once again, I need to claim the breath prayer, "You are my hope and confidence!" Let go and let God!

Chapter Five

Portion

"The Lord is my portion."
—Psalm 119:57 (NAS)

"YOU ARE MY PORTION!"

In allowing the Lord to become your hope and confidence, He can become your portion to make it through the battles of this life. A portion is the part of a whole allotted to a person or group. It's only in the Lord that our portion can become whole, complete, and perfected.

Other words that might be used in place of portion are serving and helping. This seems to be saying that the Lord is all that you need in life. You need nothing more than the Lord at the table of life, to be filled and satisfied. Many times, what you want and need to be filled or satisfied are two different things.

Dieters are encouraged to reduce their food portions and eat a little bit of everything, not a lot of anything. According to dieting theory, when you eat beyond your body's satiation limit, you reset your internal guide, as to what you need to include more and more excess. You turn up your appetite beyond what you really need to stay healthy.

Some eating experts say you need to listen to the wisdom of your body and eat what your body is craving. When your intake isn't exquisitely fine tuned to your output, you put on extra pounds that put a strain on your cardiovascular and musculoskeletal systems. Financially, when your intake isn't equal to your output, you end up in debt. The same thing happens emotionally and spiritually.

When you make the Lord your portion, everything else follows in that wake. Recently, I faced an instantly life-threatening infection that settled next to the carotid artery in the sphenoid sinus. My financial support system, emotional, and spiritual resources were not equal to the demands. When I hit the wall and claimed, "You are my hope, confidence, and portion," everything else fell into place. The Lord became my portion and brought all I needed, as I needed it!

Chapter Six

My Daily Bread

"Give us this day our daily bread."
—Matthew 6:11 (NAS)

"YOU GIVE ME MY DAILY BREAD"

When I was first diagnosed with systemic lupus erythematosus (SLE), I became shackled in the prison of my yesterdays and tomorrows. I was stuck focusing either on what horrible, or wonderful thing might come tomorrow, or how great yesterday was and longing to have it back. I was constantly obsessing about fears, anxiety, grief, anger, and fantasies, based in my past and future.

Slowly, I began to break the bars of that prison by groaning from my spirit as I woke up and went to bed each day, "Help me make it through this day; thank You for this day." My pastor pointed out that I was praying this phrase from the Lord's Prayer. That gave the feeble groanings of my spirit the structure of formal words and understanding.

At first, present moment living was only a means of survival for me. At times, it was broken down to millisecond living. By breaking what seemed to be monumental tasks into milliseconds, moments, and days, step by step, I made it through my deserts to the valleys and mountain-tops. In time, present moment living became celebration, the abundant life, to be anchored in the bread of the Lord, centered and focused in the miracle of the mountain of the moment of now!

As the children of Israel traveled through the desert, the Lord gave them just enough manna or bread for each person to have one small bowl full a day, per person. They couldn't save it, one day to the next, except on the sixth day so they wouldn't need to labor on the Sabbath. If they tried to save manna for the next day, it bred worms, and became foul. They survived on only what they needed, as the Lord provided their portion for the day.

Christ offered His body to become broken bread for you to provide the grace you need, day by day. The Lord's grace only comes in the moment, as you step out in faithfulness, to the task at hand. You can live by bread alone with the Word of the Lord. You need to harvest only your portion of fresh bread within the moment or day. You can't hoard it for the next moment or day!

Chapter Seven

God's Will

"Thy will be done, on earth as it is done in heaven."

—Matthew 6:10 (NAS)

"THY WILL BE DONE"

The next phrase of the Lord's prayer that I found myself trying to breath in the storms of illness and divorce was "Thy will be done!" I'd put unspoken exceptions, provisions, and conditions at the end. For example, if I can return to work and not need to go on disability, if this illness isn't serious and limit my activities or if Jim will come back and not divorce me.

I fought, struggled, cussed, screamed, and yelled, "No! Not this cup or that cup! Take them away!" These battle fields lasted days, weeks, months, and years. Slowly, by ever so slowly, I was able to drop my limits on what God's will might be. God's will unfolds, moment by moment, in all the events of my life. As I fight the Gethsemane battle, I pray "Thy will be done."

Friends and onlookers found it hard to believe that God's will could be found in my illness and divorce. There were those around Jesus that felt that Jerusalem and the cross, couldn't possibly be God's plan and will for Him. They were looking at things from earthly calculations, reason, and ration. None of this would compute to them from where they were standing.

Standing on the other side of the cross, you and I can see blessings, redemption, and re-creation for all mankind, the Lord's view! As you stand at the beginning of your life, you think that you can find God's will at that point for the rest of your life. Not so! God's will is that you might manifest His strength in every moment of your life to His honor, praise, and glory. The particulars matter not.

The Lord is looking at your relationship with Him in the tiniest things of life. You do God's will, not by being useful for Him, but by being in right relationship to Him. It's God's permissive will that you not wrestle with Him, but wrestle with things before Him, like Jacob.

As you abide in the Lord in every circumstance, battle, and struggle of life, you are the will of God. It's only as you obey and are faithful to the task of the moment, in the darkness and unknown, that you find the Lord's will. The Lord expects you to do His will and helps you to do it.

Chapter Eight

Deliverance

"Do not lead us into temptation, but deliver us from evil."
—Matthew 6: 13 (NAS)

"You Deliver Me"

When it seemed my whole world was collapsing around and on me, I'd find myself slipping into periods of self-pity, anxiety, fear, depression, over reactivity, hopelessness, helplessness, and despair. The battlefield of my mind would become littered with negative, unhealthy thinking. I would become obsessed, consumed, and possessed with and by these black thoughts.

It would get to the point that my thoughts would interfere with my life, living, and relationships with husband, children, friends, myself, and God. Thoughts about the circumstances of my life would become my main focus blocking out everything else in it.

For every thought you have, there is a corresponding body response in your chemical, hormone, breathing, and muscle balance. Your thoughts and corresponding body changes make up your emotions. Thoughts + body response = emotions. The Lord meant for you to use your emotions as your guide in life, not your GOD.

My illness, divorce, thoughts about them, and my mind/body feedback loop were becoming my main focus and GOD, not just my guide through life. Each would fan the other. I would be caught in a downward spiral of the mind, body, and spirit. I'd find myself desperately breathing, "give me balance." Don't let me slip and fall." Deliver me from these thoughts!"

I was praying "You deliver me!" Over and over the children of Israel were delivered from their tempting thoughts and fears on the battlefields of their history. They were tempted to run, flee, and give up when they logically looked at the odds of the battles they faced. When they added God in to the equation of their thinking, and made Him their main focus, they were delivered in every battle no matter how hopeless things looked!

Chapter Nine

Forgiveness

"Forgive us our debts, as we have also forgiven our debtors."
—Matthew 6:12 (NAS)

"GOD, FORGIVE ME A SINNER!"

Relationship problems were one of my greatest hurdles in both the divorce and illness process. Anything that is different about you, makes you threatening and overwhelming to other people. They seem to be threatened and uncomfortable around you, especially if you are uncomfortable with yourself. Many of the people around you may get stuck in denial. To acknowledge what is happening to you, raises the possibility it could happen to them.

With the diagnosis of my illness, one entire support system fell away. As divorce swept through my life, another whole system went down the drain. I'd find myself being caught in and choked by circular obsessional thoughts of judgement, anger, blame, bitterness, resentment, vindictiveness, and retaliation. The pull-away was definitely a two way street.

I can't help what thoughts come into my mind, but I can choose what I do with those thoughts and what they stir up in my body. I can process, understand, make sense of, experience, listen to, use them as a guide, and release them. I attract unhealthy, destructive consequences in my body when I focus on and make those kind of thoughts my GOD.

Slowly, I began to learn to break the vicious chain reaction cycle of thoughts that began with judging, by assuming responsibility for myself, and breathing "God, forgive me, a sinner!" I do play a part in all of this. I am not a victim, but a participant. I can choose what I focus on. I needed to do this with my vanishing support communities and with Jim, as he disappeared over the horizon of my life.

Over and over, I'm tempted to get caught up in the chains of judging myself against others, or others against me. Breathing "God, forgive me, a sinner" over and over, sets me free miraculously and instantly. This works also when the chaining thoughts are fear, confusion, doubt or when any thought or feeling becomes my main focal thought, or GOD instead of the Lord Himself!

"Forgive us our debts, as we have also forgiven our debtors."
—Matthew 6:12 (NAS)

"I Forgive"

I thought learning to assume responsible power for myself, and breathe "God, forgive me, a sinner" was a monumental battle. That battle waxed and waned over years of experience, study, counseling, and lead-

ing by the Holy Spirit. I had no idea
of what or how difficult the next phase
of the battle would be to learn to
breathe "I forgive!"

The Lord worked on me through
devotionals, Sunday School lessons,
and Bible passages. He brought Moses
before me who not only forgave the
Children of Israel for making the fat-
ted calf, but asked God to take him in
their place, if God couldn't forgive
them. Jesus forgave the soldiers at the
cross and gave himself in their place.
In neither instance were the people
asking for forgiveness, or had a sense
of their sin, but they were forgiven.

The Lord pointed out that I'd be
forgiven, in like manner, as I had forgiven. I certainly didn't want to forgive if it meant that I had to love and
leave myself open to being hurt again.
But the Lord said "yes" to both. The
Lord showed me that forgiving was
simply a matter of taking my place in
front of the cross along with those I
felt had wronged me. I became a sinner on level ground with everyone
else.

Standing in front of the cross as a beautiful sinner, human being, lost and broken child of God made me whole in His redeeming love. That allowed me to forgive and let those who'd hurt me stand in equal status at the Savior's feet. Forgetting was not required, just remembering who and where I was.

Forgiving was for me and not the other people. As long as I am trapped and stuck in judging, anger, blame, bitterness, vindictiveness, and retaliation, I can't assume responsibility for myself and the power to change myself to move on in my life. I can only be free, as I ask for and give forgiveness, before the throne of the cross of the Lord!

Chapter Ten

Praise

"Hallowed be Thy name."
—Matthew 6:9 (NAS)

"PRAISE, HONOR, AND GLORY BE TO YOUR NAME!"

Prayers of thanksgiving, praise and joy are hard to come by when you are in the midst of the battles of life like illness, divorce, and death, financial survival! Praise may filter in only on an occasional basis through the pleas for strength, deliverance, protection, and survival. Praise seems to be reserved for periods of celebration rather than battle.

The Lord led me through the Psalms several times to show me how the Psalmist would claim the blessings of God in praise, descend into his valley of battle, and then mount up once again on the wings of the Lord's glory. The Psalmist was embracing the dark side and the light side of life, to find his wholeness, as Jungian psychology challenges you to do.

To truly embrace the wholeness of the Easter experience, you need to give thanks and praise for noon on Friday, as well as sunrise and Easter morning! In the chaos of the feeding of the five thousand, Jesus lifted what little there was to heaven and gave thanks and praise to find the miracle of the abundance to feed the crowd!

When you shut down on part of yourself, you shut down other parts of yourself, too. Without the rain, you'd have hard baked soil where nothing could grow. To see the rainbows you need to face the storm with the Son behind you. You need to embrace all of life, giving thanks and praise to the Lord in it all.

This is another breath prayer I fought and still fight with all my might. The Lord has led me to begin every prayer I pray, with, "Father God, I give you thanks and praise for my life and everything in it!" At night, I list everything in my prayer journal that has occurred that day and give thanks and praise. The Lord inhabits my praise and thanksgiving and makes me over.

Chapter Eleven

The Kingdom

"Thy Kingdom come."
—Matthew 6:10 (NAS)

"THY KINGDOM COME"

The Lord's Kingdom and King-ship needs to come rule in all parts of your life, whether it's illness, divorce, family, work, pleasure, money, or whatever. It is totally amazing and awesome to me to look at the areas of my life where the Lord's Kingdom has come and is coming daily.

His Kingdom has come and is coming in my illness and produced healing on many levels: a series of books and articles, a counseling ministry, and speaking around the country on living with chronic and terminal illness.

His Kingdom has come and is coming in my divorce as I have returned, studied, and found healing from what I went though in my marriage and divorce, in marriage and family counseling, and passing it on in my family, counseling ministry, speaking, and writing.

His Kingdom has come and is coming in my dysfunctional family, as my denial dissolves, reality floods in, and I work my recovery process from codependency, and communicate what I learn in my relationships, counseling ministry, writing, and speaking.

Matthew 6:33 encourages you to "Seek ye first the Kingdom of God and His righteousness and all these things will be added unto you." The Kingdom of God is everything within us. Righteousness is right relatedness to God, yourself, and others. The rest of life will flow from this focus as His Kingdom comes!

I have come to feel that The Lord's Kingdom coming in every relationship of my life, to myself, God, and others is what life is really all about. The rest of life is just the trimmings and structure by which that can happen. It all begins by asking the Lord to let His Kingdom come and rule in all domains of your life.

Chapter Twelve

Redemption

"My grace is sufficient for you."
—2 Corinthians 12:9 (NAS)

"My times are in Your hand."
—Psalm 31:15

**"IN YOUR PERFECT
GRACE AND TIMING."**

As my life was going through mayhem, and it seemed nothing could ever go right again, the Lord seemed to pierce through my heart, soul, body, and out into eternity, the promise, "In My perfect grace and timing, I will redeem all things!" Through the cloud and fog of the chaos of all that was happening, I'd breathe over and over, "In Your perfect grace and timing."

The reference to time in the Psalm doesn't mean clock-time. The Psalmist is referring to those momentous times in our lives like birth, marriage, death, getting sick, and getting well, the Lord showing you sparks of beauty and understanding, and a sense of life jelling or taking a new direction. These events are like eternity breaking into time with moments of unforgettable deep meaning.

God's time is on an eternity timetable. Eternity begins with the moment of now and unfolds a day at a time. You and I want to know the itinerary for the rest of our lives. I want to have all the answers now! . . . if not 15 minutes ago. Patience is not one of my virtues, especially when in crisis.

I was diagnosed with SLE in 1978. When my book, *Successful Living with Chronic Illness . . . Celebrating the Joys of Life* came out in 1985, I began to see evidence of the Lord's redemption of this part of my life in His perfect grace and timing. I could see it only in looking back and not in the moment. I am learning to claim the Lord's redemption way beyond what I can imagine, dream, or guess in the event and moment, even when I can't see, what it is.

All I do is follow one bread crumb at a time, turn over every rock in my path, and be faithful to the task of the moment, to eventually be able to look up and see just a fraction of the Lord's redemption in His eternal timing. Many times I have thought that I was just whistling in the dark and really going nowhere. Suddenly, I'd look back and see God's perfect grace and timing is taking me somewhere on my journey home to Him!

Chapter Thirteen

The Way to Walk

". . . Teach me the way in which I should walk; For to Thee I lift up my soul."

—Psalm 143:8 (NAS)

"I'll Know the Way to Walk as I Lift My Soul to You."

Many times I get so bombarded with the circumstances of life that I don't know which way to turn or what to do. Things may be coming at me from all directions, overwhelming me. I am so caught up in the fray and frenzy of things that I can't see the forest for the trees.

This breath prayer helps me shut up the babble of my nonproductive, drunken monkey of a mind, to be able to step back, detach, and see things more clearly. When you are so close to a situation, you can't see the intricacies and nuances, or the big picture of what's happening, to be able to make a wise, healthy decision. You may react from an unconscious gut level in a knee-jerk manner.

You may regret your reaction when you get back from the situation and can see it more clearly. Detaching with this breath prayer helps you avoid codependent tendencies, to be emotionally fused and enmeshed. You can then consciously make deliberate decisions and choices from your head and heart.

Using this breath prayer has literally given me hindsight in the situation so that I don't do, or say, something that I regret later. I am able to see the forest and the trees, as well as the foreground and the background. There's no way I can see all the things that are in motion in an event. I can only trust that to the Lord.

Lifting my soul to the Lord is such a beautiful image. The Lord can shine His light through my soul and onto my circumstances to help me see more clearly than I ever could on my own. With both screens of reality in view, the Lord can protect and show me the way to walk, avoiding snares and pitfalls that I would never see or recognize.

Knowing Myself

"For now we see through a glass darkly; but then face to face: Now I know in part; but then I shall know even as also I am known."

—1 Corinthians 13:12 (KJV)

"I Will Know Myself as I am Known"

It seems fitting that the end results of the love chapter in I Corinthians 13 is that you will know yourself as you are known. If you love as this chapter describes, with long suffering, kindness, no envy, ego void state, no unseemly behavior, no self gain, a long fuse, no evil thoughts, rejoicing in truth, dependability, and bears, believes, hopes, and endures all things, you will know yourself, as you are known.

All through life you need mirrors to be able to see yourself to maintain balance, adjust your path, and respond appropriately. Your body has a whole system that provides you with a mirror, called proprioception. This system gives you feedback that helps you maintain an awareness of your extremities and body position. Without this feedback or mirroring system, you would not be able to maintain physical balance or coordination.

The emotional mirrors that may have been provided to you by your care takers in growing up, may have labeled you with unhealthy, destructive, unrealistic perceptions, and conceptions of yourself. You may not have been given an image of yourself that needs to stay balanced and coordinated emotionally in life. You may have been called stupid, dumb, foolish, sweet, funny, bad, or other things. You may have been given double signals by what was said and what was acted out in a way that left you confused and conflicted.

The greatest gift that could have been given to you as a child would be love that is described in this chapter, unconditional love. In the mirror of this love, you would have seen yourself as a beautiful child of God. You would have been cherished, protected, and nurtured. No matter how good a parent is, you come into life with some childhood wounds and breaks. You try to find healing for the rest of your life.

As I see myself as a child of God, in the mirror of God's love, I am able to heal the childhood wounds and breaks that I bring into life with me. I can drop the defenses that keep the denied, repressed, and suppressed parts of myself under wraps. I can begin to know and love myself, as I am known. I can embrace all of myself, to find the abundant life! The dark glass becomes the clear mirror of the Lord's love!

Chapter Fourteen

Love

"You shall love the Lord your God with all your heart, and with all your soul, and with all your mind, and your neighbor as yourself."

—Luke 10:27 (NAS)

"MAY YOUR LOVE FLOW THROUGH ME!"

Just as this is the greatest commandment, it is also the greatest breath prayer. I say it to myself as I fall asleep, as I awaken, and when I am meditating. It's at these times that the unconscious mind is most open to suggestion from the conscious mind. I feel like I am consciously re-writing the unconscious tapes of my mind, focusing on God's love.

You can't love like the love described in I Corinthians 13 without first loving yourself in the flow of God's love. I can only love myself in a healthy balanced way, as that love is centered in the flow of God's love, healing, filling, and sealing me. It's only when the flow of God's love is my base of support and foundation that I can then turn and love myself, anyone else, or life in a healthy, balanced way.

It's only in these loving relationships that I can learn about and get to know God, myself, and others, to His honor praise, and glory. I believe in getting to know, learn about, and embrace God, yourself, and others. This is what this life is all about. The rest of life is just the trimmings and structure by which you can do this.

I feel I have a lot to learn about myself from anyone that I am attracted to, male or female. Opposite sex attractions are particularly fertile areas for growth and understanding. Supposedly, you are attracted to someone who has the repressed, denied, and suppressed parts of you. You are repulsed by someone who is similar to you.

Jesus promised that if you seek His Kingdom, which is everything within you, and His righteousness, which is being in right relationship with God, yourself, and others, everything else will fall into place. Relationships found in the flow of God's love are where the real juices of life are.

In the flow of God's love, I become congruent with myself. I am at one with myself. Congruent means that I don't split myself by feeling one way and acting another, or thinking one thing and saying another, just to please someone else. I find "at-one-ment." I am at one with myself in the moment. I am whole when I am centered and focused in the flow of God's love.

The end results of I Corinthians 13 is, that I will know and see myself, as I am known and seen. That's truly being congruent. I respond to others and make choices in life from a realistic knowledge base of myself. When I spilt myself to please someone else, I loose my internal navigational guides and take the wrong path.

I felt I lost some of my prestige and authority when I moved my counseling practice out of a doctor's office and into my home. I thought framing all my academic certificates, diplomas, and awards and putting them on my office wall would make me feel more official and bolster my ego.

Finally, I framed I Corinthians 13 and hung it in the middle of all of my diplomas and certifications. I realized that all of those other pieces of paper were meaningless without the credential of God's love flowing through me. My ego is swept aside in the flow of God's love and becomes the force in my life.

I find an ego void state as I am emptied out and filled with God's love through the Holy Spirit. When I become ego involved with anything or person in my life, I become that thing or person. Stress and wounds that originate in the ego are washed away, as my ego is flooded with and displaced by the flow of God's love.

A vast body of understanding is emerging from the study of dysfunctional families and the codependent relationships that come out of them. Codependent relationships invariably involve some form of addiction that is mood altering, to fill an empty emotional cup, quell anxiety, or numb pain.

An addiction can take on many different forms. The flow of the love of the Lord needs to be the only thing that I depend on to fill my overflowing emotional cup. Then I don't need to compulsively seek any addictions or addictive relationships to alter my mood and take care of my anxiety.

I have found many miracles happening in my life as I pray "May your love flow through me." I am finding recovery from my codependency. My denial is crumbling away to see myself more clearly. I am learning how to take care of myself and break the triangle of codependency where everyone becomes a victim.

I am learning how to listen to myself, stay congruent, by clearly and directly setting my boundaries, and asking for what I need assertively. I don't leave it up to someone to be able to read my mind or a crystal ball.

The reality of realistic expectation is being centered and focused in the flow of God's love, when trying to love in a relationship, saves much destructive behavior for all involved. It's only in the flow of God's love that healthy relationships can be found or founded.

It's only in the flow of God's love that you can love yourself enough, in a healthy balanced way, so that you can then love your neighbor as yourself. You can't give what you don't have. If you are full to overflowing in the flow of God's love, you can give from a full cup rather than try to fill your cup in codependency care taking.

"I love Thee, O Lord, my strength."
—Psalm 18:1 (NAS)

"You Are My Strength To Love."

In a stressful situation, the first thing that you do is to doubt and tear yourself down. At first, I thought that "You are my strength to love" meant that the Lord is my strength to love others, but then I realized He is my strength to love myself. In loving myself in the flow of God's love and strength, I can love anybody, or handle any situation!

The Lord brings people to you that you need to learn things from about yourself. People that rub you the wrong way usually remind you of yourself in some obscure, or not so obvious way. The Lord brings people to us to show you how you have been and are to Him. You are attracted to people who have the parts of yourself that you have repressed or suppressed in your efforts to survive your childhood wounds.

You are attracted to people who you feel like will heal your childhood wounds. You need the presence, guidance, protection, counsel, and leading of the Holy Spirit to walk through these relationships. The love of God is given to us by the Holy Spirit. "The love of God has been poured out in our hearts by the Holy Spirit who was given to us" Romans 5:5 (NAS). God's love flowing through you is given by the Holy Spirit and manifests itself spontaneously.

The Lord seems to have given me a love mandate when I love someone. In order to love, reach out in love without any promise of what will come back in return; release the person to be where they are, wherever that may be; be congruent with whatever I am feeling and thinking in the moment; pray for the person and ask them to pray for me; share and praise what God's doing in my life; do all of this in the flow of God's love and Him, as my strength to love.

I can't focus on or try to figure out where the flow of God's love may be taking me. I need to focus on being faithful to the mandate in the moment of now. God doesn't call me to success. God calls me to be faithful to the process in the present moment. He'll take care of the rest!

In doing this, no matter how crazy it may feel, the flow of God's love will carry me either to, or beyond, that person. In the process, He will help me to learn what I need to learn from that attraction to find more wholeness and healing. Doing this is like loving into the dark and unknown. I have found it to work and keep me alive to the flow of God's love!

With the Lord as my strength to love myself, I am learning how to set my boundaries and ask for what I need assertively, clearly, and directly without being wimpy, whining, complaining, aggressive, nagging, or combative. The assertive sentence is a healthy balanced loving way to ask for what I need, and to set my boundaries.

With the assertive sentence map, I frame my understanding of where the other person is with, "I understand that you . . . ," frame what I need as an "I" statement with, "but I want, feel, like, need, or think . . . ," and negotiate for what I need, or set a boundary, with the last part of the map. To use the assertive sentence map, I need to have a sense of where the other person is and what my real needs are, so that I don't address just surface issues.

I negotiate from an ego void stance of loving myself and that person in the flow of God's love. It's the force and energy of God's love flowing through me that makes it possible for me to know what I need and what boundaries I need to set. I don't scream, yell, cry, and pout with "you" statements while, using the bony pointing finger of blame. I assume my own power and responsibility for myself, with "I" statements.

I feel the assertive sentence map embodies the Martial Arts approach to handle an attack and also expresses what Jesus meant by turning the other cheek. I turn my cheek and head to go with the blow of the attacker so the blow glances off of me. I throw my attacker off balance in allowing the full force of the blow to just graze by me.

I stand firmly, solidly, and calmly where I am with the assertive response. I may need to ask repeatedly, with my assertive sentence, as I am centered and focused in the broad base of support of the energy of God's unconditional love energy flowing through me.

To be able to use the assertive sentence map with "I" statements in a healthy, loving way, the Lord needs to be the source of your loving yourself. The flow of God's love allows you to not need to scream, yell, cry, or pout. You can let go of "you" statements and retire the bony pointing finger of blame.

You can let go of the unrealistic expectations that other people should know what you want or need by crystal balling and mind reading . . . "They should, ought, must know what I need and want!" This leads to judging.

To be able to assume responsibility for yourself and use "I" statements; you need to individualize, differentiate, and find your free-standing emotional identity, separate from anyone, or anything else in life. You can do this only in the flow of God's love.

Differentiation includes separating from emotional fusion with others, as well as emotional and intellectual fusion within yourself. When you reach greater levels of differentiation, you are less emotionally reactive to others and your life.

Emotional fusion can be recognized when you see someone who is: clinging and dependent, especially for long periods during and following a crises; aloof and isolated; unable to firmly and calmly hold many convictions and beliefs; constantly seeking approval and acceptance above any other goal; unable to make rational decisions or have many opinions; dogmatic or compliant; prone to inflate themselves or attack others when stating their beliefs.

Finding your identity as a child of the King in the flow of His love helps you to find your own identity, differentiate, and assume responsibility for yourself. You are able to respond to life and others from your heart and your head, rather than react destructively from your gut. You can ask for what you need with clear, direct, assertive "I" statements as many times as it takes.

You are set free to make conscious decisions and responses, not just unconscious reactions. You can need someone because you choose to love them in the flow of God's love, rather that love someone because you need them. You can make love a choice!

"May your love flow through me!"

I am finding, for God's love to flow through me, that I need to prepare myself to be an open vessel by going back and daily working the steps of the Lord's Prayer to allow the flow of God's love through me. Other parts of the Lord's Prayer are the results and outcome of working those steps.

There are four major steps to work the program of the Lord's Prayer. First, I need to pray "God, forgive me a sinner." I assume responsibility for myself . . . the beginning of emotional, physical, and spiritual health.

Second, I need to turn to those on level ground around me before the cross and say, "I forgive."

Third, I need to give the Lord thanks, praise, and glory for my life and everything in it, the good, the bad, the laughter, the tears, the rain, and the sunshine. "Hallowed be Thy name." Fourth, I need to surrender to God's will, whatever it may be, trusting that He redeems all things in His perfect wisdom, grace and timing.

The results of working the steps of the Lord's Prayer and God's love flowing through me are:

1. "Give me this day my daily bread."

God's love becomes the flow and source of my energy, healing, leading, guiding, and sustenance moment by moment—fresh daily bread!

2. "Lead me not into temptation but deliver me from evil."

God's love flowing through me becomes my protection so that I am able to: set boundaries; know what I need and ask for it specifically, clearly, directly using assertive "I" statements;

and avoid self-destructive behaviors and damage.

3. "Thy kingdom come."

The authority and power of the rule of His Kingship will be manifested in every area of my life . . . my relationships, counseling, family, writing, divorce, speaking, illness, and everything! His Kingdom will come in ways that I could never begin to imagine, fantasize, or dream of!

"The steps of a good man are ordered by the Lord."

—Psalm 37: 23 (KJV)

"May your love flow through me to order my steps."

Love is energy. God's love is the greatest source of energy available. God's power is greater than the power of a ferocious hurricane bombarding a coast, a tornado's mighty fury, or a bloom of a tender flower bursting through the earth's hard crust.

With God's love flowing through me, I have that much power and might at my disposal to love and live life. "Your perfect love casts out my fear" I John 4: 18 (NAS).

May Your love flow through me to order my steps, serve as a guide and energy to carry me down the river of life, to lead and direct me when I am lost, to heal parts of my broken self, to bless and protect me.

Sometimes, I feel like I am finding my way through life by Braille on my hands and knees. I fumble, stumble, fall, and crawl into each day. I am picked up and carried through the day by being open to the flow of God's love pouring through me.

As God's love flows through me, I see myself becoming a crystal. The light of God's love is refracted and reflected through me. The full spectrum and beauty of the hues of the rainbow fall on those around me in red-oranges, yellows, greens, blues, and purples, without my even knowing it.

As God's love flows through me, I find His order in my life, step by step. His order is no pain, tears, suffering, death, or disease. His permissive will is all of these. As I am open to the flow of His love and find His order, in each step of every day, miracles happen.

I am finding there is an unbroken circle in the flow of God's love from God to me to others. If I try to block the love flow at any point because of pride, fear, or anger, I break the circuit, damage, and block the flow within myself. I hurt and stall the motion within me.

God's order in your life is that you bring honor, praise, and glory to His name by being in right relationship to God, yourself and others, whatever the circumstances of your life. You can find this order only as the flow of God's love orders your steps.

Each morning as I wake, I stay in bed an extra amount of time praying over and over on the perfect breath "May your love flow through me to order my steps." I don't want to get ahead of or behind that flow. Either way, I'll crash and fall. I need to stay right on the crest of the wave of the flow of God's love, to take me through this journey of life on my way home to Him.

Chapter Fifteen

Healing

"Bless the Lord, O my soul; And all that is within me bless His Holy name! . . . Who heals all my diseases."
—Psalm 103:1, 3 (NKJV)

"IN CHRIST'S NAME YOU HEAL ALL MY 'DIS-EASES!'"

You can have dis-eases on many levels, mind, body, or spirit. A disease in your mind may cause a disorder in your body and spirit. A "disease" in your spirit can cause problems in your mind and body. A "disease" in Your body can cause a disturbance in your mind and spirit.

The prefix "dis" before a word means negation, lack, removal, rejection, or distance from the thing that follows it. The noun, ease, means the condition of being without discomfort, freedom from pain, worry, agitation, difficulty, hard work, great effort, or financial difficulty. So the word "disease" means to be without all of the above described conditions or states.

The word, heal, means to become whole. In the sermon on the mount, Jesus said, "You shall be perfect, just as your Father in heaven is perfect" Matthew 5:48 (NKJV). The word perfect means whole, complete, balanced. In these verses, perfection and healing are linked to loving, even your enemies.

Just about every treatise written on healing gets to the topic of loving. Learning to love God, self, and others is essential to healing. Dr. Larry Dossey in *Healing Words* says, "Love is intimately woven with health. The power of love to change bodies is legendary, built into folklore, common sense, and everyday experience" (p. 109).

Research has shown that loving actually increases immune function. Love helps you transcend the body and logical mind. Only love from God shared among others can generate the healing fire. Loving in the flow of God's love allows you to let go of judgment, anger, and fear, the chains that bind you.

The powerful energy of God's love flowing through you can wash away the ravages of 'dis-eases' of the mind, body, and spirit. Love can relax your breathing and muscles, stimulate a hormone soup, lift your spirit, put a song on your lips and in your heart, radiate as a glow from your face, even make you dance.

In praying for the healing of another, you may find healing for yourself. Giving love back to God in praise and thanksgiving can bring healing. Healthy love that emanates from the mouth of the river of God's love can balance the thoughts of your mind, tune the timing of your body. and give rebirth to your spirit.

Sometimes the greatest 'dis-ease' you can have is in your thoughts. Every thought translates into changes in the hormonal, chemical, immune, muscular, and respiratory systems. I imagine this is why so much attention is given to thoughts in the Bible. Every thought you have is manifested in your body in some way.

If you have a 'dis-eased' mind or thoughts, you're definitely going to have a 'dis-eased' body and spirit. Changing a thought to a breath prayer scripture affirmation can bring the Holy Spirit into its temple, your body, and give the Holy Spirit His sword, God's Holy Word, and open your spirit to the Holy Spirit's presence. Healing of all your 'dis-eases' can begin to occur on a mind/body/spirit level!

Chapter Sixteen

Thoughts

*"The Lord knows the thoughts of man.
That they are futile."*
— Psalm 94:11 (NKJV)

"You Know My Thoughts."

Only 10% of your mind and thoughts are known to you. Ninety percent of your thoughts is in the unconscious mind. Interesting that the Lord requires 10% of your earnings. Stands to reason that He'd also want 10% of your thoughts.

Using breath prayers as you're falling asleep, waking, and meditating enables you to expose your unconscious to the scriptures and the Holy Spirit. Saying breath prayers as you go through the day can harness your conscious thoughts and maybe bring up some of the unconscious into the conscious.

A lot of times, you may not even know what you were thinking about when you do something. You may end up asking yourself "What in the world was I thinking? Why on earth did I do or say that?" Sometimes, you may not know what to think in a situation, or in certain circumstances. Your thoughts may get scrambled, overloaded, and confused. The Lord knows all of your thoughts.

Study has shown that some thoughts lead you to depression and others lead you to stress. Some study has discovered the possibility to certain thought patterns that may lead to physical illness. Your thoughts and physical manifestations of those thoughts can translate into illness, disease, and pain.

As I counsel people, I can see how and when thoughts have been played out metaphorically in their bodies. I have been able to see it in myself. If I can locate where my thoughts are being manifested in my body, I can claim "In Christ's name You heal all my dis-eases." In time, I'll get in touch with the thoughts that were the root cause.

Satan tries to get hold of your thoughts and enter the door of your mind and life. Daily battles are fought in your mind, victories are won, and conquests lost. Satan does some of his best work with judgment, anger, doubt, and fear. He can catch us quickest with those kinds of thoughts.

In Louise Hay's book, *You Can Heal Your Life*, she has put together a compilation of thought patterns that she feels cause specific physical problems. I like to take her work, identify a thought pattern, and then, take that into a scriptural breath prayer affirmation.

It's so wonderful to think that the Lord knows my thoughts, both conscious and unconscious. The Lord can heal all my "dis-eased" thoughts that produce a troubled spirit and a sick body, even when I don't know what my thoughts are.

When I recognize, block, and re-place "dis-eased" thoughts with breath prayers, I can find wholeness and healing of mind, body, and spirit level.

The Lord can take my futile thoughts and put His thoughts in their place. No matter what my circum-stances, I can choose my thoughts about those circumstances.

Chapter Seventeen

Peace

"You keep him in perfect peace, whose mind is stayed on YOU."
—Isaiah 26:3 (NKJV)

"You Keep Me In Perfect peace."

When your mind is stayed on the Lord, it remains or continues in a given place or condition. Your mind stays in one place and doesn't just run from thought to thought like a drunken monkey with no direction or anchor. When your mind is swinging from thought to thought, you're dragging your body with your thoughts.

With thoughts running wild dragging the body behind them, you are truly "dis-eased," in mind, body, and spirit. You can be at ease, at rest, and at peace when Your mind is stopped and then focused on the Lord. It's only when your mind is thrown out of gear and shut off that your body can relax.

Stopping your thoughts and then staying your mind on God, no matter what waves are lapping around you, keeps you in perfect peace. I don't think I can even imagine what perfect peace is. The only definitions I have at my disposal of peace are all centered around the absence of something like war, hostilities, quarrels, and disagreements.

Somehow, the peace that's mentioned in the Bible is not just an absence, but more of a presence, an addition, a completing. In John 14, Jesus describes the peace He's going to leave the disciples. It's not like anything that this world knows. Your heart won't be troubled or afraid.

It doesn't say that everything will be perfect, or that there'll be an absence of war, murder, illness, suffering, and death. There will be the addition of peace with all of those things. You'll transcend the things of this world to find a peace of mind this world can't give.

Christ coming into your life can be anything but peaceful on this earthly plane. The first thing that Christ does is destroy every peace in your life that is not based on Him. The early Christians certainly didn't know peace in their circumstances but knew unbelievable peace in their minds that were stayed on God. They had peace even as the lions approached to devour them, chained in jail, or had their families ripped from them.

Jesus rebuked the waves with, "Peace, be still!" They immediately responded. Peter had the peace to walk on the water, as long as he kept his vision, mind, and focus on Jesus. As soon as his vision, mind, focus, and thoughts drifted, he sank in the waves.

Keeping your mind stayed on the Lord takes a conscious concentrated effort, minute by minute, and thought by thought. It takes catching yourself in unhealthy thinking, willing yourself to stop those thoughts, and then replacing them with thoughts of the Lord—breath prayers.

"The peace of God, which passes all understanding, will guard your hearts and minds through Christ Jesus."
                    —Philippians 4:7 (NKJV)

"YOUR PEACE GUARDS MY MIND."

It seems that the mind is the gateway for the Holy Spirit or Satan to gain access to your life. Your thoughts are so automatic and fire so rapidly that you may not even be aware of from where they came. You make a mistake, like any other human being and immediately you may be calling yourself stupid or dumb.

You may do something and say to yourself "Why on earth did I do that? What was I thinking of? I must be crazy!" Your thoughts translate into actions, bodily changes, and decide your life's direction.

Your mind needs a guard in order to protect you from Satan. This

Scripture says that the peace of God will guard your heart and mind through Jesus Christ. In Isaiah, it says that you will be kept in perfect peace when your mind is stayed on the Lord. The forgiveness given by Jesus Christ brings an extra measure of peace that can guard your mind.

Jesus forever takes away judgment and judging. So many of your thoughts can be snared by judging yourself or others. Judging wraps chains of bondage around you. Thoughts of judgment and judging can lock you in the chains and bondage of obsessional thoughts.

Christ took away all judging by bringing forgiveness and teaching you how to forgive. Peace usually is used in the context of the absence of war or conflict. War and conflict usually involves judgement and judging of some sort. War and conflict can be internal or external.

War and conflict, in the outside world, can be an indicator of war and conflict on the inside. The sequel to judging is anger, blame, bitterness, vindictiveness, and retaliation. This chain of emotions has been played out, over and over, in history and in people's lives.

For there to be real peace, there needs to be forgiveness and acceptance of yourself, then you can forgive and accept others. You can only do this forgiving and accepting through the forgiveness and love that Jesus brings. The peace that Jesus brings passes all understanding.

Since the beginning of time, there seems to have been war and rumors of war. It's beyond your understanding to even conceive of a time of complete peace within and without. You can't have peace in the world until there is peace within the people of the world.

Jesus came to give the peace that takes away judgment and judging. Suspending judgment guards your mind from being caught in that destructive chain to you and all around you. Only the peace that Jesus gives can guard your heart and mind.

Chapter Eighteen

Infirmities

"I will rather boast in my infirmities, that the power of Christ may rest upon me."

—II Corinthians 12:9 (NKJV)

"YOUR POWER RESTS ON ME."

Sometimes, I wonder how I can boast in my infirmity. How can I boast about pain, fatigue, fever, or nausea. I usually think about complaining, or talking about them, but boasting! You usually would boast about victories, accomplishments, material possessions, or success, not illness or weakness.

So often, illness is looked on as a failure or punishment, not something to boast about. People avoid you when you talk about your illness. They just can't handle it. They run, give choice pieces of advice, suggest treatments or cures, tell you it'll all be okay or you're strong and you can handle it. Some people will keep any weakness or illness secret, for fear of people's responses.

It's interesting that the physical infirmity that Paul asked the Lord to remove three times seems to have been an eye problem that wasn't painful, but maybe made his appearance repulsive. For three days after Paul was struck down on the road to Damascus, he lay blind not eating or drinking.

Some people feel the "thorn in the flesh" that Paul asked the Lord to remove may have been a vision problem.

Paul's response was that he'd boast in his infirmities so that Christ's power would rest in him. I found that when I was first diagnosed, I talked about my illness in an endless exhibitionistic manner. This is normal behavior when you're in crisis. My manner was one of confusion and searching, certainly not boasting.

I began to notice that I talked more about my lupus than I ever did about my Lord. For a while, lupus was my God because it had become the main focus of my attention. I deliberately tried to start balancing that out and talk more about the Lord than lupus.

Paul didn't name his thorn in the flesh or infirmity. Once when I was asking for prayer at a healing service, I noticed I didn't need to go into the gory details, or even name the illness. That was new for me and a healing all by itself. At one time, telling people I had lupus was secondary only to telling them my name.

Victor Frankl says that you can choose your attitude or what you think, no matter what your circumstances. I can choose to think about my symptoms and complain, or I can think about my illness and the Lord's presence and power, and boast in it! Brag about my lupus, what a thought!

"I will rather boast about my weaknesses, that the power of Christ dwell in me."

—II Corinthians 12: 9 (ASV)

"YOUR POWER DWELLS IN ME."

An infirmity can be of the mind, body, or spirit. Webster defines infirmity as lack of power, disability, bodily debilitation, frailty, or moral weakness. Boast is defined as to brag about one's accomplishment, talents, or possessions with excessive pride.

The computer of my brain is teased by putting infirmities and bragging together. I wouldn't logically put the two together, just the opposite, or backwards, of what I would normally think. It seems the Lord does His best work with the illogical, impossible, and unlikely. He uses a stable, cross, weakness, and infirmity to bring about His best work.

It's hard for me to even imagine how to practically go about doing this. Paul says speaking with pride about your lack of power, disability, bodily debilitation, frailty, and moral weakness allows the power of Christ to dwell in, or rest upon me.

Dwell means to reside, remain, fasten one's attention, exist in some state, or place. He whose mind is stayed on me, I will give perfect peace, peace beyond your understanding! I come the closest to doing this boasting when told I'm so strong, by responding, "No, 'In my weakness is Christ's strength manifested.'" This verse talks about power not strength.

You usually think of power in earthly terms coming from position, money, or strength. Webster defines power as strength, forcefulness, effectiveness, might, authority, the ability to exercise control, or might. None of these definitions make any reference, even remotely similar to an infirmity.

The Lord's power is shown in a stable, cross, hurricane, tornado, cascading waterfall, fragile flower nosing its way through the hard earth, beating heart, lost soul redeemed, and other illogical ways. It's shown in ways you and I can't even imagine.

All that aside, how do you, in practical terms, boast or brag about your lack of power, disability, bodily debilitation, frailty, or moral weakness? It seems that in following Paul's example, you don't necessarily mention what the infirmity is, then go on and on about it. Whatever your infirmity, mind, body, or spirit, you need to brag about it. Paul bragged, "I am the worst of sinners."

Paul seems to say you make reference to the fact that you are struggling with an infirmity without giving it much attention of glory, just brush by it. Don't deny the enormity of what you're dealing with. In bragging about, or boasting in your infirmity, you don't bog down in or get stuck in it.

You move quickly on to saying that you can't handle this alone. God's power dwells in, or rests upon you as you brag about this infirmity. Bragging about the infirmities of your life is the door through which the Lord's power can enter, dwell in, and rest upon your life.

Appendix A

The Theory

Everyone experiences stress. Distress is when your perceived stress is greater than your perceived resources.

Some of the resources that maybe you used to cope with stress in the past may be lost: health, spouse, friends, family, physical outlets, or financial resources. These losses and grieving them are actually a part of the crisis itself.

You feel overwhelmed and perceive you are left with a resource deficit. You are left with a mountain of problems. You view your resources as being inadequate to deal with the stress you are facing.

Resources that have been shown to help deal with stress are: self-disclosure, self-directedness, confidence, acceptance, social support, financial freedom, physical health and fitness, stress monitoring, tension control, structuring, problem solving, cognitive restructuring, functional beliefs, and social ease.

A major life crisis generates many little daily hassles that translate into a great deal of stress. You seem to have the least number of resources to deal with stress at a time, when the greatest number of stresses come.

Stress theory postulates that adding in two uplifts for every hassle helps you balance out the effects of stress in your life. Every breath prayer is an uplift. At 14 breaths a minute, you have the potential for 20,160 breath prayers a day. That can balance out most any stress you're experiencing.

In going through many major life crisis experiences, the Father is teaching me how to pray without ceasing, using breath prayers. Using breath prayers as a resource arms me with the perception of tipping the stress resource balance back in a positive direction. I feel at flow with myself.

I am only now beginning to realize all the sound psychodynamic approaches and Psychoneuroimmunology theories that breath prayers incorporate. I sensed they were powerful in my life. I am only now beginning to understand why.

Stress Spiral

The effects of stress build up and are stored in the body over time. You wake up and can't find what you want to wear. You go up on the stress spiral to a 10. You recover to 5. You go in the kitchen and drop an egg. You are stressed to 15. You recover to a 10. There's a wreck on the freeway, up to 20 and back to 15.

You go up the stress spiral throughout the day. A normally neutral event, that you ordinarily might not respond to, sends you out of the ceiling, when you are already tight from stress. You start out at an even higher level of stress. You go even higher on the stress spiral with the next stress.

Your chances of ever descending the stress spiral escalator to recovery and ground zero again decrease with each successive stress. You need to build a program into your daily life to achieve stress recovery.

You can work at stress by reducing the number of stress factors in your life, altering your reactiveness to stress, and sloughing away stress toxins stored in the body. Breath prayers incorporates each of these approaches to stress and adds in the rocket boost of the power of the Holy Spirit. The following theories help explain why breath prayers are so powerful.

Meditation

The use of meditation goes back some 7,000 years in history. Most religions advocate some form of meditation. The key element in all meditation techniques seems to be breaking the racing thoughts of your mind.

Thoughts produce physiological arousal in your body to give you emotions. Every thought manifests in hormonal, chemical, breathing, muscular, and immune system changes in the body. The body's response escalates your anxious thoughts and then, in turn, stirs up more in the body by way of the mind\body feedback loop.

Meditation is similar to staring into space. Your mind is thrown out of gear like when you are driving a car alone, and don't remember a stretch of the road. That out of gear state is attained, intentionally, and maintained for a period of time with meditation.

Attention is focused on a mantra or phrase that has little arousal or meaning for you as you exhale. Feverish obsessional thinking is slowed down or blocked. A calmer, more centered, and focused rather than fragmented and scattered consciousness is produced.

Your spirit and body are united in a sense of wholeness and presentness. The "noise" of life is quieted. You hear your own spirit, only when you shut off the racing thoughts of your mind. The body can't relax unless the mind is knocked out of gear or turned off. Your mind is at work, even while you sleep.

It has been shown that during meditation the body's basic metabolic rate is reduced 16 to 17%. Carbon dioxide elimination increases. The respiratory rate decreases. Oxygen is used more efficiently. Blood lactate levels that produce anxiety are decreased.

Heart rate and blood pressure both drop. Galvanic skin response decreases, reflecting a decreased metabolic rate. All the stuff that is stirred up in the body from the stress of your thoughts slows down. These physiological changes carry over to other times in the day. Your response to stress is reduced and blunted. The effects of the stress spiral in the body are sloughed away.

You become less reactive to stress. It takes more to send you sailing through the ceiling. You, also, get a physiologically conditioned reflex response. Your body is trained to relax automatically in other situations, when repeating the mantra used in meditation.

There are other equally impressive psychological responses. People who meditate respond to stress just like anyone else. They recover from stress arousal better and don't get caught in the stress spiral. The full effect of meditation won't be felt until it is used one to two times a day for ten to twenty minutes for a month. The effects of finding recovery from the stress spiral are cumulative.

There seems to be a greater sense of aliveness and responsiveness. You pay less for feeling so alive. Daily, you are unloading your stress baggage on a mind and body level. You are getting in touch with your own spirit at the same time.

In Eastern thought, meditation broadens perception, allowing the person to "get outside" the ego. The need to be important is decreased. The need to be important is often a big source of stress. Through meditation, a greater sense of self-love, celebration of life, patience, perspective, and lessened agitation may be generated. A sense of peace results.

Indians think of the mind as a drunken money. It produces useless thoughts and internal noise that excludes awareness. Meditation gets you past the ego, quiets the chatter of life, and opens you to a new awareness of the universe.

I found that attaining a level of deep muscle and breathing relaxation and meditation for 20 to 30 to 60 minutes a day, promote emotional growth, new thoughts, self-acceptance, and understanding. I found myself growing emotionally and spiritually, by leaps and bounds, after I began meditating.

I have worked with patients whose emotions were very bound in their bodies. They would have accelerated growth and understanding as they began doing deep muscle and breathing relaxation and meditation. Working on a mind, body, and spirit level accelerates personal growth.

Sometimes traumatic, suppressed, and repressed memories and emotions from the past surface in very dramatic ways when you begin meditating. Feelings that are trapped and held in the body are released as the body relaxes. Daily meditation helps you process and stay current with your emotions.

Using breath prayers with deep muscle and breathing relaxation and meditation techniques, programs my body to relax at the signal of a scriptural affirmation. The effects of meditation are multiplied as the extra power of faith and the intervention of the Holy Spirit is added in.

I condition, nourish, and process myself on a mind, body, and spirit level during meditation with breath prayers. I continue my workout using the same breath prayers throughout the day, wherever I am, or whatever I am doing. Daily use of breath prayers in both arenas empowers the breath prayers, as I see and experience the results and benefits.

It's like opening the flood gates of my mind, body, and spirit to allow the calming, centering, and focusing flow of the Holy Spirit's presence. Using breath prayers in meditation gives the potential for going deeper into the self and attaining greater heights than I would have ever imagined possible.

Psychoacoustical and Self Hypnotic Meditation Tapes

Psychoacoustical and self hypnotic meditation tapes deliver complicated sound and frequency patterns to the auditory areas of the brain. The result is a wide band of "neurological stimulation." This stimulation facilitates the integration of new information.

The tapes use metaphors. Metaphors are the language of the unconscious mind. There is much less resistance to metaphors and the unconscious mind hears the message in them. A metaphor creates a greater chance for change.

I open myself to deeper levels of my unconscious mind by using psychoacoustical tapes during my time of deep meditation and relaxation while breathing breath prayers. Breath prayers are metaphors in their truest sense.

Breathing Exercises

The natural rhythm of breathing is interrupted when you are stressed. You may breathe too fast, (hyperventilation) or too slow (hypoventilation). With hyperventilation, breathing is rapid and shallow, resulting in increased oxygen intake and decreased carbon dioxide. Dizziness, weakness, numbness of an extremity, nervousness, and many other frightening physical responses may result.

With hypoventilation, oxygen intake is decreased. Carbon dioxide is increased. Increased oxygen makes the body too alkaline. Increased carbon dioxide creates an acid state in the body. The body is at its best somewhere in between the two states of balance.

Under stress, you unconsciously may change the chemical balance of your body by the way you breathe. The perfect breath is a one to two ratio. You inhale through your nose to the count of three and pull the breath deep into your gut with abdominal breathing. You exhale through your mouth to the count of six. You balance out your breathing with the perfect breath. Reaching normal breathing patterns reduces high arousal. The feeling of distress is relieved.

The philosophy of yoga contends that the mind is the master of the senses, while the breath is the master of the mind. The use of breathing exercises results in strengthening and conditioning your pulmonary system, enhancing your cardiovascular function, promotion of oxygenation, and calming of your nerves. Calmness results.

The reticular activating system (RAS) is the part of your brain that filters any stimuli reaching the brain. It decides whether a stimuli should go any further or be blocked. It's like a "security system" for the brain. The breathing centers in the brain have a close relationship with the RAS. Constant, steady, restful breathing promotes relaxation.

In addition to promoting neuromuscular relaxation, breathing exercises also play a vital role in the prevention of respiratory ailments. Breathing exercises can help vitalize your lungs' functioning and regulate your breathing patterns.

Respiratory reserves are built up and the body's ability to get oxygen to the blood and body is increased. Prescribed breathing techniques will restore your body to its natural balanced pH condition and relieve nervousness and anxiety.

In the creation story, the Lord breathed in the breath of life. The very root of inspiration is the word inspire. You "in"-"Spirit," or breathe in the spirit. Being alive and sensing your aliveness involves breathing in deeply and exhaling.

With breath prayers, you breathe and open yourself to the inspiration of the Holy Spirit. You exhale the fatigue, pain, confusion, and brokenness, while claiming a scriptural promise as an affirmation to heal it all.

Using the perfect breath with breath prayers the body is allowed the right to balance itself, chemically, in mind, body, and spirit. Inspiration is found as you inhale and exhale.

Cognitive and Rational Emotive Therapy

Your thoughts stress you more than anything else in life. What you think about an event or circumstance will drastically alter your experience and perception of it.

The body's only interpretation of your environment comes from what you think about it. Thinking stressful thoughts gears up the body for stress, just as if you are actually in a stressful event.

The physical response to stress is exhibited by tense, contracted muscles, resulting in an accumulation of pyruvic and lactic acid; sweating; increased blood pressure, pulse, and respirations; an increase in the supply of blood sugar and fat to the muscles and brain; dilated pupils; blanched skin; and excretion of norepinephrine into the system.

You can be anticipating or remembering a stressful event. You gear the body up, just like you are actually experiencing the event, by thinking about it. Your thoughts may escalate even more in response to your body's arousal in a mind\body feedback loop cycle.

Obsessively replaying anxious thoughts, reliving, or catastrophizing an event, arouses and stresses your body. Your body doesn't know the difference between an event and your thoughts about the event. There is no physical outlet for the stress stirred up in your body by your thoughts.

It has been found that observers of a stressful event experience more stress than those actually participating in it. You experience less stress if you physically act out your thoughts and bodies' responses of fight or flight. You can't fight or run from so much stress you experience in our modern world. You can only choose what you think about it.

Thought-stopping is a process in which you deliberately try to break the viscous cycle of obsessional circular thoughts. You catch yourself beginning to get on the thought escalator.

You deliberately interrupt the thought by saying, "Stop!" or visualizing a beautiful, pleasant scene. You continue to break the cycle, until it remains broken, no matter how many times the method has to be used. This can be a powerful tool, but it does take practice.

I have found breath prayers add a powerful dimension to thought-stopping. In addition to breaking up the negative thought patterns, a positive scriptural affirmation is put in their place. I short-circuit my destructive, negative, death-giving, obsessional, circular thoughts, and their effects on my body by repeating a breath prayer.

The power of my mind, body, and spirit are harnessed to move in the direction of health, healing, balance, and wholeness. I find health, life, energy, and direction from positive life-giving scriptural affirmations. My thoughts are focused and opened to the breath of the Holy Spirit.

Thought hygiene has been found to be a powerful tool in fighting depression. Your moods are a direct by-product of your thoughts. If you are depressed, your thoughts are mostly negative. You see the world through dark lenses. Your negative thoughts usually contain some mistaken thinking.

The first step is to learn to recognize your negative thoughts and catch yourself in the act. Then you can begin to challenge, eliminate, and replace the negative thoughts with positive healthier thoughts. You can begin to deal with your depression more effectively.

Your thoughts are automatic and unconscious. They come from your family of origin programming. You're not even aware when they hit your brain. Your body registers these thoughts in an exquisite monitoring system.

You can't recognize these thought patterns until they have been red-flagged for you. Listed below are ten of the most prevalent kinds of negative thinking.

1. All-or-nothing thinking: Things are seen as being black or white. There are only extremes with nothing in the middle. "I am either all good, or all bad" but not a mixture of both. One experience, negative or positive, may unrealistically color your total outlook on life, or self-perception.

2. Over generalization: One single negative event may be seen as a never-ending pattern of defeat.

3. Mental filter: You pick out one negative part about yourself, or your life and dwell on it exclusively. It darkens the rest of your vision of reality. When you are depressed you block out anything positive.

4. Disqualifying the positive: When you are depressed and something positive happens, you ignore or dismiss it as not being significant. You aren't able to embrace or absorb a compliment, good news, an award, success, victory, or achievement. You dismiss it as a fluke, or maintain that it doesn't count.

5. Jumping to conclusions: Mind reading: You assume you know how people are feeling and what they are thinking about you, without checking it out. You may then react by withdrawing, or counterattacking when the person's actions may have nothing to do with you.

Fortune teller error: You imagine negative or bad things about to happen and foretell only misery for yourself. You take this as a fact and act on it, even though it may not be based on reality.

You avoid a friend and feel angry if they don't return a call, rather than check to see if they may not have gotten your message. You see one lab test foretelling gloom and doom.

6. Magnification (catastrophizing) or minimization: You either blow things out of proportion, or shrink them, depending on which end of the binoculars you are looking through. You magnify your errors, fears, limitations, and imperfections and exaggerate their importance.

You may magnify other people's positive or good points. You minimize and play down anything good or positive about you. Inferior feelings are guaranteed to follow.

7. Emotional reasoning: You use your negative feelings as the only test of reality. If I feel this way, it must be this way. With depression, things feel so negative for you that you assume that they are that way. You come to conclusions based on your negative reasoning that aren't based on reality.

8. Should statements: "Should, ought, must, and have-to" are used to motivate yourself from external expectations or internal tapes from your past. You aim these statements at others or yourself. There is

usually pressure to perform or resulting resentment.

Performance anxiety that results from this kind of thinking can cause problems in everything from sleep to sex to making a speech in public. Self-hate, shame, and guilt are by-products of should statements. Realistic expectations of yourself, the world, and others helps put these in order.

9. Labeling and mislabeling: As an extreme form of over generalization, you may, in anger, apply a label to yourself or someone else. The label is usually a judgment response to the self or other's behavior that colors your reactions to yourself or others. I'm a "pig," he's "insensitive" or "uncooperative."

10. Personalization: You assign yourself great powers to control not just influence others. You assume responsibility for negative events, even when there is no reason for doing so. You blame the responses of other people on your sense of inadequacy, rather than allowing them to be responsible for their own actions. You feel crippling guilt and carry the weight of the world on your shoulders.

Once you have caught yourself in, identified, and challenged your negative thoughts, you can choose to replace them with a positive scriptural affirming breath prayer. The nonproductive drunken monkey of the mind is stopped from uselessly, obsessively, and destructively swinging from one thought to the next. Your wandering, obsessive circular thoughts lead your mind and body only into chaos and confusion.

Breath prayers give you a chance for new creative thoughts to emerge. They provide a vehicle to harness your mind and fulfill the admonition to "think on these things" (Philippians 4:8) from morning to evening. Feelings of being fragmented and scattered are replaced with feelings of being focused and centered on the Lord. "I will keep him in perfect peace whose mind is stayed on me" (Isaiah 26:3).

Pain Theories

Distraction strategies or attention-diversion help you maintain your sense of control and self-efficacy, even under stressful circumstances. The focus of your attention affects the amount of awareness of a stimulus that you have.

A painful experience can be modified by what you focus your thoughts on. You can minimize both physical and emotional pain and increase tolerance of a situation by shifting and manipulating the focus of your thoughts.

When you focus on and become preoccupied with physical and emotional pain, it may limit what you feel you can do or talk about with others. Continually focusing on and complaining about pain tends to decrease pain tolerance and increase the awareness of pain.

Constantly talking and complaining about pain may become an indirect unassertive means of asking for what you need from people without directly asking them. You may get to the point that it takes being in pain or getting sick before you can ask for what you need.

It is healthy and normal to focus on, attend to, and process your emotional or physical pain a certain amount of time. You need to understand, feel, make meaning of, get it in perspective, and experience it fully before you can release it to move on. You tend to process emotions in segments and pieces. To process it all at one time, isn't really possible.

Trying to hide or ignore pain only puts the spotlight on it. The best way to remember something is to try to hide or forget it. You waste a lot of energy trying to hide or ignore pain. Pain is a signal you need to listen to but not let it become your only focus or god. Your pain can be your guide to a brighter tomorrow.

There have been times when I have felt drained, confused, fatigued, and pained. I'd think I couldn't possibly put one foot in front of the other. I listen to those cues and respond appropriately to them but don't make them my main focus or god.

I attract more fatigue, pain, and confusion when I make them my obsessional focus. Using breath prayers to distract me from the difficulty, whether physical or emotional, spiritually I'm helped to not foolishly expend my physical or mental energy. Suddenly, I find what I thought was impossible has become possible.

Attention can be like a spotlight that accentuates the object on which it is focused. Everything else drops into the shadows. The dark will appear unclear, distant, and irrelevant. Focusing totally and obsessively on your pain enlarges and empowers it.

I listen to my pain and let it be one of my guides but not my god. I choose to make scriptural promise affirmations my main focus, after I process the pain, anger, and anxiety in every way that I can. Breath prayers have been a potent distraction from emotional and physical pain. Breath prayers focus and distract me away from the pain. They attract the power and healing of the Holy Spirit to me.

Scientists think that you can reduce pain by blocking or closing a "pain gate" located in the spinal cord. The supposed "gate" decides whether or not a pain signal from the body will actually reach the brain, where it is recognized as pain.

According to the Gate Control Theory of pain, attention focus is one of the main influences that widens the "gate." Any inhibition of pain messages rising to the brain is prevented by not focusing on the pain. You partially close the "gate" and diminish the pain sensation experienced by distracting your focus.

The Gate Control Theory also suggests that pain can be alleviated by inhibitory signals from the cerebral cortex and thalamus in the brain itself. Thoughts, emotions, and past experiences housed in the brain produce impulses that affect the transmission of pain impulses to the brain.

Your experience of pain is influenced by your interpretation of it. Information about your pain, a sense of control, anxiety, and depression affect your pain. Pain can be relieved by decreasing anxiety and increasing a feeling of confidence.

Stress, dwelling on pain, and fatigue open the pain gate. Using heat or cold at the site of the pain, physical therapy, and a positive attitude close the pain gate. Breath prayers can block my pain at the spinal "gate" and brain level. They close the pain gate and open my mind to go beyond the pain.

Internal and External Locus of Control

Having a sense of control seems to be a potent mediator in reducing and enhancing your ability to cope with stress. You may feel that your life is controlled by events outside of yourself with the external locus of control. Fate, chance, other persons, and circumstances have more power over what happens to you than you have. You see yourself as powerless and with no control.

You feel you can direct your own destiny and make your own decisions and choices with an internal locus of control. You feel you have the power to influence your world and make things different.

You need to combine both the internal and external locus of control to find a healthy balance. It is healthy to realize, realistically, that there are some things that you can influence and change. There are some things that you can't control. The "Serenity Prayer" expresses this well . . .

"God grant me the serenity to accept the things I cannot change, the courage to change the things I can, and the wisdom to know the difference."

No matter what my circumstances, I still have the freedom to choose my attitude. I exercise the control of the effects of circumstances over me in choosing my attitude. Using breath prayers enhances my freedom to choose my attitude and strengthens my internal locus of control.

Strangely enough, breath prayers, also, help me to realize, in a healthy way, that there are things within my life, circumstances, and environment over which I have no control. I reduce my sense of helplessness, felt in an external locus of control mode, by giving ultimate control to God through the Holy Spirit.

I am able to live "The Serenity Prayer." Trying to be rigidly controlling, or helplessly giving up all control can waste a lot of energy. I combine the internal and external locus of control by connecting my spirit with the Holy Spirit to find limitless power and strength.

Neurotransmitters

Neurotransmitters, such as endorphins and serotonins, are the bodies' natural mediating healing substances. It has been found that the body can more judiciously secrete these pain and mood altering substances when the body is in a relaxed state or at flow.

Many pain medications work by closing the pain gate. Sensation is blocked from the brain. Scientists now know that the brain and spinal column can release endorphins that close the gate and relieve pain.

By centering, focusing, and calming myself with breath prayers, I help my body use these natural substances in their own innate wisdom. The guidance and wisdom of the Holy Spirit is an added factor to the healing wisdom that lies within the body itself.

Presentness

You can imprison yourself in the moments of yesterday and tomorrow. You are not free to experience the moment of "now." You can shed a great deal of anxiety and anger by becoming focused on the present moment. You don't try to stretch yourself ahead or back in time. You no longer get ahead of yourself and trip over yourself. You avoid getting beside yourself and out of your mind.

The present moment is the only real thing that you have. Everything else is only an abstraction. One of the ways that you can fight being immobilized is to learn to live in the present moment. You find the joy and celebration of the abundant life, only by fully living in the present moment.

Breath prayers constantly drag, center, and focus me before the Lord in my present moment. I find myself not getting ahead of myself, beside myself, or out of my head. I avoid tripping myself up. I am fully present and accounted for. I live in the present which is beautiful. It stretches beyond the limits of the past and the future.

Detachment and Transcendence

In breaking codependent patterns of relating, you need to learn how to detach from an emotional situation. Detachment helps you gain some emotional distance, objectivity, and perspective. Detachment isn't cutoff, but gaining just a little emotional distance.

You can respond from your head and heart in healthy loving ways with some emotional distance. You don't react in unconscious, gut, knee-jerk, unhealthy ways. You can see the forest and the trees, the background and the foreground, in all, the whole picture.

I find that with breath prayers I can do more than detach. I find that I actually transcend the situation. I not only can pull back slightly from the situation but I also pull just slightly above it. Using breath prayers, I find that I am able to have insight in a situation that is almost equal to hindsight!

Autogenetic Suggestion and Imaging

It has been found that through imaging and autogenetic suggestion you can actually help your body combat illness such as cancer. You can learn to control bodily functions through autogenetic suggestion and imaging.

You can start with controlling muscles and move to actually control the functioning of organs. You can learn to control circulation to a limb, lower blood pressure, and even control insulin levels. Biofeedback enhances this learning.

Cancer patients are encouraged to image their white cells and chemotherapy killing off offending cancer cells, while in deep relaxation and meditation. Startling results have been found. Patients with a poor prognosis have unexpectedly fought off what was thought to be terminal cancer.

Imaging can be used to relieve and control pain. Imaging can also improve an athlete's performance. POW's have come home to play a perfect golf game, after imaging their game during their imprisonment. Your body doesn't know the difference between the thought or image and the real thing.

I have a hard time coming up with and staying focused on images. I do better with, and feel I have found many mini-healings, by combining focusing on, and intensifying areas of physical, emotional, or spiritual pain, while breathing a breath prayer, claiming healing during deep relaxation and meditation. Emotional and spiritual pain are uniquely, physically manifested in each individual.

I'll image a person's face, an issue, or any area of dis-ease. I focus on, picture, and feel any dis-ease in the mind, and locate where it manifests in the body. I intensify and enlarge the dis-ease of the mind, body, or spirit, and lift into the Holy Spirit claiming healing in a scriptural promise as an affirmation.

I feel lifting and enlarging any dis-ease while claiming a spiritual promise of healing and balance is more powerful than any imaging or autogenic suggestion that I can ever imagine. I don't have the wisdom to know what to image, or suggest to my mind, body, or spirit on the level of the Holy Spirit.

I do a head to toe spiritual MRI (Magnetic Resonance Imaging), as I do my 30 to 45 to 60 minute meditation and deep relaxation each day, using psychoacoustical or self hypnosis tapes. I start with my head and go down my body, while breathing, "You heal all my diseases" or "I am light and health as Your Spirit flows through me." I'll meditate more times in a day, when feeling worse.

I can tell exactly where any infection, inflammation, muscle tension, or dis-ease is on a mind, body, or spirit level. I'll stop and focus on those areas for a while. In the next segment of the meditation, I'll breathe, "May Your Love flow through me," imaging the river of God's love flowing through the dis-eased parts or areas of my emotional, physical, or spiritual being.

Up until the modern era of technology, healers knew that the mind, body, and spirit were intimately and intricately interwoven and connected. The role of ancient healers was to find and tap into the healing potentials within the mind, body, and spirit of each person.

The Lord has given you everything within that you need to find healing. Our scientific age has taken the focus and responsibility away from the individual. The power of healing has been assigned to medical technology, practitioners, and institutions.

You are never told you have healing power within you, much less taught how to tap into or use it. No matter how much knowledge we as health care professionals accrue, we will still be "practicing" medicine. The real wisdom, power, and healing resides in the mind, body, and spirit of each individual.

You need to learn how to dig your own personal wells and descend into the river of wisdom that flows through the ages in all of us. Until then, your attempts at healing will only be marginal and fragmented.

You need to be responsible for and learn how to take care of yourself. You need to develop a daily program that conditions you on an emotional, physical, and spiritual basis to find healing, balance, and recovery, on a moment by moment basis.

I feel breath prayers work much the same way that antibiotics and anti-inflammatory medications do. Antibiotics don't kill an infection. They just retard the growth of any bacteria, until the body can martial an attack to kill off the bacteria.

Anti-inflammatory drugs just cool off inflammation, which is a by-product of the immune attack. The body, in its own wisdom and healing, decides when to call off the immune system. I feel breath prayers lift my damaging mind up off my body to allow it to do its own intuitive healing under the direction of the Holy Spirit.

I break the mind/body feedback loop spiritually. I keep my mind from abusing my body with obsessional, anxious, or angry circular thoughts. I get off the stress spiral escalator. I lift it all to the Holy Spirit.

The effects of breath prayers is cumulative, additive, and ongoing. They take on a life of their own. I make the Great Physician my resource for ultimate healing and wholing on all levels. "You are my hope and confidence" (Psalm 71:5).

Coping Response

Research shows that the way you cope with stress-influences affects the way stress is processed in your body. Two distinct and different ways of coping have been identified and documented by physiological and behavioral research. Active coping and passive.

Passive coping with helplessness, hypervigilance, and conservative withdrawal seem to lead to a hormonal body response. The passive coping hormonal route leads to elevated hormones, immune system suppression, and mental depression. A downward spiral can, eventually, lead to physiological imbalance and illness.

Active coping seems to kick the body into a healthier neurochemical body response. Neurotransmitters have been shown to be released differently in stressful situations, accompanied by active coping responses. Mood levels and pain are, thereby, modulated by the way you cope.

Breath prayers tap into my active coping response. I deliberately identify, attack, and challenge my faulty thinking that can lead to passive coping and degeneration of my body. I replace deathgiving, destructive thoughts and subsequent behaviors with lifegiving ones.

I fine tune my body, mind, and spirit. I find balance, wholeness, and health a spiritual rebirth and recreation, breath by breath. I get off the upward, mental, stress, spiral escalator and avoid a downward physical spiral. I get on the up escalator of life guided by the Holy Spirit to transcend life where I am.

Anxiety Management Training

Anxiety management training is similar to systematic desensitization used to treat phobias. Anxiety management training doesn't require the involved component analysis of systematic desensitization to determine the stages of the phobic reaction. With anxiety management training, the entire anxiety producing scenario is dealt with at one time.

The person identifies scenes that create anxiety and scenes that elicit deep relaxation for them. You practice deep relaxation with deep breathing, while focusing on the relaxing scene. While relaxed, you switch to the anxiety producing scene.

Physical manifestations or cues associated with the anxiety are noted. These cues are identified and become signals in the future to focus on the relaxing scene. Periods of practice, switching back and forth, between the scenes are rehearsed in therapy sessions. Then you encounter the real thing and experiment with the technique.

Breath prayers are a unique form of anxiety management that aids in the spiritual and faith systems. Breath prayers dramatically address the thoughts producing the anxiety, the body manifestations, and bring in the blessing of the Holy Spirit. An abstract relaxation scene is fortified with a concrete, scriptural promise as an affirmation in anxiety producing circumstances.

Affirmations

Affirmations can be used to help reprogram the unconscious mind. When you are at the edge of sleep, as you wake in the morning, or go to sleep at night, is the time you have the greatest access to the unconscious mind. Repeating positively framed affirmations, at these times of the day, can have a powerful affect.

The conscious mind, also, can easily access the unconscious mind during meditation. During meditation, new understanding can be introduced. New windows of your mind can be opened to allow new insights, thoughts, and wisdom.

Deep painful areas of your life, which you have exerted a lot of unconscious energy to suppress, may surface to be healed and released. You are bound by but can't release feelings until you feel, go through, experience, make some sense of, and understand them.

You have the opportunity to rewrite the unconscious messages of your mind by breathing scriptural affirmations, during meditation, as you're falling asleep, and waking. What better way to give over to the Holy Spirit the conditioning of 90 to 95% of your unconscious mind. You focus the 5 to 10% of your conscious mind on scriptural promises to reprogram the tapes of your unconscious mind.

Breath prayers are simply claiming a scripturally based spiritual promise as an affirmation. You repeat it on the exhaling of the perfect breath, on waking, falling asleep, in deep meditation, as you experience or walk throughout your day. It is an aerobic mental, physical, and spiritual workout!

Conclusion

Breath prayers quiet the useless, obsessional, nonproductive, and circular chatter of my mind. When I focus on God, I find perfect peace instead of being pulled in many different directions by my mind. With my mind turned off, my body can relax, and find its own perfect healing sources and resources. The Lord has given everything within me that I need to find healing, wholeness, and balance.

With breath prayers, I shut off the wounding of my mind and open up to the relaxation and healing of my body and spirit. I descend the deep wells within myself, to find the river of wisdom and healing that flows through the ages. Using breath prayers opens me to the infilling of the Holy Spirit.

I find new creative thoughts bubbling within me. My spirit quickens and stirs within me. I can hear, trust, follow, and act on the wisdom of my inner spirit. My spirit can also hear the whispering, wisdom, insight, and leading of the Holy Spirit!

Breath prayers are not in any way meant to replace therapy, counseling, or medical treatment. I have found breath prayers potentiate and empower all other conventional forms of treatment, far beyond what they could accomplish by themselves.

Prayer without Ceasing
by Kathleen S. Lewis

Breath prayers are turning a scripture into a seven syllable affirmation, and saying it on the perfect breath. Breathe in to a count of three and out to a count of six. The following are examples of Breath Prayers by topic. This listing is by no means exhaustive of the vast, rich supply of breath prayers in the Bible. I only begin to scratch the surface here.

Affliction

"Your word comforts me in my affliction," (NAS) Psalm 119:50.

Anxiety

"You try and know my anxious thoughts," (NAS) Psalm 139:23.

Boldness

"In you I have boldness and confidence," (NAS) Ephesians 3:12.

Broad Place

"You bring me to a broad place," (NAS) II Samuel 22:20.

Clay

"You bring me out of the miry clay," (NAS) Psalm 40:2.

"You are the Potter . . . I am the clay," (NAS) Isaiah 64:8.

Comfort

"Your word comforts me in my affliction," (NAS) Psalm 119:50.

Compassion

"You crown me with lovingkindness and compassion," (NAS) Psalm 103:4.

Confidence

"You are my hope and confidence," (NIV) Psalms 71:5.

"In you I have boldness and confidence," (NAS) Ephesians 3:1.

Darkness

"You illumine my darkness" (NAS) II Samuel 22:29

Defense

"You are the defense of my life," (NAS) Psalm 27:1.

Delight

"You delight in me," (NAS) II Samuel 22:20.

Deliver

"You are my deliverer," (NAS) II Samuel 22:2.

"You deliver me from my strong enemy," (NAS) II Samuel 22:18.

"You deliver me from the strivings of my people," (NAS) II Samuel 22:44.

"Your lovingkindness delivers, helps, and saves me," (TLB) Psalm 109:21-26.

"You deliver me from lying lips," (NAS) Psalm 119:2.

"You deliver me from all my fears," (NAS) Psalm 34:4.

"You deliver me in a day of trouble," (NAS) Psalm 41:1.

Discernment

"You teach me discernment and knowledge," (NAS) Psalm 119: 66.

Distress

"You relieve me in my distress," (NAS) Psalm 1:4.

Encourage

"You answer and encourage me," (TLB) Psalm 138:3.

Enemy

"You deliver me from my strong enemy," (NAS) II Samuel 22:18.

"You save me from my enemies," (NAS) II Samuel 22:4.

Faith

"You are the author and perfecter of my faith," (NAS) Hebrews 12:2.

Fear

"I'll not fear for You are with me" (NAS) Isaiah 41:10.

"You deliver me from all my fears," (NAS) Psalm 34:4.

Feet

"You make my feet like hind's feet," (NAS) II Samuel 22:34.

"My feet do not slip," (NAS) II Samuel 22:37.

"You don't allow my foot to slip," (NAS) Psalm 121:3.

Free

"You set me free from the snare," (NAS) Psalm 124:7.

Future

"You give me a hope and a future," (NAS) Jeremiah 29:11.

Grace

"Your grace is sufficient for me," (NAS) II Corinthians 12:9.

Grief

"Your word strengthens me in my grief," (NAS) Psalm 119:28.

Guard

"You guard my going in and going out," (NAS) Psalm 121:8.

Guidance

"Your hand guides, strengthens, and supports me," (TLB) Psalm 139 10.

"Your counsel guides me," (NAS) Psalm 73:24.

Hand

"Your hand of blessing is on my head," (TLB) Psalm 139:5.

"Your hand guides, strengthens, and supports me," (TLB) Psalm 139:10.

"Your hand leads me," (NAS) Psalm 139:10.

"You hold my hand," (NAS) Psalm 37:24.

"I am the work of Your hands," Isaiah 64:8.

Heal

"You heal all my diseases" (NAS) psalm 103:3.

Hear

"You hear my cry for help" (NAS) Psalms 22:24, II Samuel 22:7.

Heart

"You enlarge my heart," (NAS) Psalm 119:32.

"You search, know, and test my heart and thoughts," (NIV) Psalm 139:23.

Help

"You help me," (NAS) Isaiah 41:10.

"You hear my cry for help," (NAS) Psalms 22:24, II Samuel 22:7.

"Your help makes me great," (NAS) II Samuel 22:36.

"Your lovingkindness delivers, helps, and saves me," Psalm 109:21-26.

"You are my help and shield," (NAS) Psalm 115:9.

"You are my present help in trouble," (NAS) Psalm 46:1.

"You hasten to my help" (NAS) Psalm 71:12.

Hiding Place

"You are my hiding place and shield," (NAS) Psalm 119:114.

Hold

"You uphold me with Your right hand," (NAS) Isaiah 41:10.

Hope

"You are my hope, lovingkindness, and abundant redemption," (NAS) Psalm 130:7.

"My hope is in Your word," (NAS) Psalm 130:5.

"You give me a future and a hope," (NAS) Jeremiah 29:11.

"You are my hope and confidence," (NAS) Psalm 71:5.

Integrity

"I stand in my integrity in You," (NAS) Psalm 26:1.

Intercession

"I hedge and lift _____ to You," (NAS) Psalm 139:5 & Romans 8:26-27.

Know

"You search and know me," (NAS) Psalm 139:1.

"Every moment You know where I am," (TLB) Psalm 139: 3.

"You search, know, and test my heart and thoughts," (NIV) Psalm 139:23.

"You know what I need," (NAS) Matthew 6:8.

Knowledge

"You teach me discernment and knowledge," (NAS) Psalm 119:66.

Lead

"You teach and lead me," (NAS) Psalm 27:11.

Life

"You are the defense of my life," (NAS) Psalm 27:1.

Lift

"You lift and conceal me in trouble," (NAS) Psalm 27:5.

"I hedge and lift _____ to You," Psalm 139:5 & Romans 8:26-27.

Light

"Darkness is light to You," (NAS) Psalm 139:12.

"You are my lamp," (NAS) II Samuel 22:29.

"You are my light and salvation," (NAS) Psalm 27:1.

Love

"May your love flow through me," (NAS) Matthew 22:37-39.

"You give me a spirit of power, love, and a sound mind," (NKJV) II Timothy 1:7.

"May your love flow through me to order my steps," (NAS) Matthew 22:37-39 & Psalm 37:23.

Lovingkindness

"Your lovingkindness is before my eyes," Psalm 26:3.

"Your lovingkindness delivers, helps, and saves me," Psalm 109:21-26.

"You crown me with lovingkindness and compassion," (NAS) Psalm 103:4.

"Your lovingkindness revives me," (NAS) Psalm 119:159.

"You are my hope, lovingkindness, and redemption," (NAS) Psalm 130:7.

Lying

"You deliver me from lying lips," (NAS) Psalm 120:2.

Need

"Know what I need," (NAS) Matthew 6:8.

Order

"May Your love flow through me to order my steps," (NAS) Matthew 22:37-39 & Psalm 37:23.

Pardon

"You pardon all my iniquities," (NAS) Psalm 103:3.

Path

"You chart the path ahead of me," (TLB) Psalm 139:3.

Perfect

"You perfect that which concerns me," (KJV) Psalm 138:8.

Pit

"You bring me out of the pit," (NAS) Psalm 40:2.

"You redeem my life from the pit," (NAS) Psalm 103:4.

Plans

"You work out Your plans for my life," (TLB) Psalm 138:8.

Portion

"You are my portion," (NAS) Psalm 119:57.

"You are my inheritance, portion, and cup," (NAS) Psalm 16:5.

Potter

"You are the Potter . . . I am the clay," (NAS) Isaiah 64:8.

Power

"You increase my power," (NAS) Isaiah 40:29.

"You give me a spirit of power, love, and a sound mind," (NKJV) II Timothy 1:7.

"You give me power," (NAS) Isaiah 40: 29.

"You have power over all things," (NKJV) Matthew 28: 18.

"Your power will save me," Psalm 138:7.

Praise

"You are worthy of praise." (NAS) II Samuel 22: 4.

Presence

"You are with me," (NAS) Isaiah 41:10.

"Your hand of blessing is on my head," (TLB) Psalm 139:5.

"You are with me when I wake," (NIV) Psalm 139:18.

Protection

"You deliver me from my strong enemy," (NAS) II Samuel 22: 18.

"You are my rock and fortress," (NAS) II Samuel 22:2.

"You are my shield," (NAS) II Samuel 22: 3.

"You are my stronghold and refuge," (NAS) II Samuel 22:3.

"You protect and keep my soul," (NAS) Psalm 121:7.

"You hedge me behind and before," (NKJV) Psalm 139:5.

"You shield me as I take refuge in You," (NAS) II Samuel 22:31.

"You give me the shield of Your salvation," (NAS) II Samuel 22:36.

"You are my deliverer," (NAS) II Samuel 22:3.

Redeem

"You redeem my life from the pit," (NAS) Psalm 103:4.

"You are my hope, lovingkindness, and redemption," (NAS) Psalm 130:7.

Refuge

"You are my rock of refuge," II Samuel 22:3.

Relief

"You relieve me in my distress," (NAS) Psalm 1:4.

Rescue

"You rescue me," (NAS) II Samuel 22:20.

Rest

"You tell me where to stop and rest," (TLB) Psalm 139:3.

Revive

"Your word revives me," (NAS) Psalm 119:25.

"Your righteousness revives me," Psalm 119:40.

"Your lovingkindness revives me," Psalm 119:159.

"You revive me in the midst of trouble," Psalm 138:7

Righteousness

"Your righteousness revives me," (NAS) Psalm 119:40.

Rock

"You are my rock and fortress," (NAS) II Samuel 22:2.

"You are my rock of refuge," (NAS) II
Samuel 22:3.

Salvation

"You give the shield of Your salvation,"
(NAS) II Samuel 22:36.

"You are the horn of my salvation," (NAS)
II Samuel 22: 3.

"You are my light and salvation" (NAS)
Psalm 27:1.

"You are my strength, song and salvation,"
Psalm 118:14.

Save

"You save me from my enemies," (NAS) II
Samuel 22:4.

"You save me from violence," (NAS) II
Samuel 22:3.

"You save me in my affliction," II Samuel
22:28.

"Your lovingkindness, helps, delivers, and
saves me," (Psalm 109:21-26.

"Your right hand will save me," (NAS) Psalm
138:7.

"Your power will save me," (TLB) Psalm
138:7.

Search

"You search and know me," (NAS) Psalm
139:1.

"You search, know, and test my heart and thoughts," (NIV) Psalm 139:23.

Shepherd

"You are my shepherd," (NAS) Psalm 23:1.

Shield

"You are my shield," (NAS) II Samuel 22:31.

"You are my help and shield," (NAS) Psalm 115:9.

"You give me the shield of Your salvation," (NAS).

"You are my hiding place and shield," (NAS) Psalm 119:114.

Sleep

"You give to me in my sleep," (NAS) Psalm 127:2.

Snare

"You set me free from the snare," (NAS) Psalm 124:7.

Song

"You are my strength, song, and salvation," (NAS) Psalm 118:14.

"You give me a new song of praise," (NAS) Psalm 40:3.

Sound Mind

"You give me a spirit of power, love, and a sound mind," (NKJV) II Timothy 1:7.

Steps

"You enlarge my steps under me," II Samuel 22:37.

"May your love flow through me to order my steps," (NAS) Matthew 22:37-39 & Psalm 37:23.

Strength

"You strengthen me," (NAS) Isaiah 41:10.

"In my weakness is Your strength," (NAS) II Corinthians 12:9.

"You give strength to the weary," (NAS) Isaiah 40:29.

"You gird me with strength for battle," (NAS) II Samuel 22:40.

"You strengthen and help me," (NAS) Isaiah 41:10.

"You increase my strength," (NAS) Isaiah 40:29.

"You renew my strength," (NAS) Isaiah 40:29.

"Your hand guides, strengthens, and supports me," (TLB) Psalm 139: 10.

"You are my strength, song, and salvation," (NAS) Psalm 118:14.

"You make me bold with strength in my soul," (NAS) Psalm 138:3.

"You give me the strength I need," (TLB) Psalm 138: 3.

Support

"You are my support," (NAS) II Samuel 22:19.

"Your hand guides, strengthens, and supports me," (TLB) Psalm 139: 10.

Sustain

"You take my burden and sustain me," (NAS) Psalm 55:22.

Teach

"You teach and lead me," (NAS) Psalm 27:11.

"You teach me discernment and knowledge," (NAS) Psalm 119:66.

Thought

"You understand my thought from afar," (NAS) Psalm 139:2.

"You search, know, and test my heart and thoughts," (NIV) Psalm 139:23.

Trouble

"You revive me in the midst of trouble," (NAS) Psalm 138:7.

"You bring me safely through trouble," (TLB) Psalm 138:7.

"You preserve my life in the midst of trouble," (NIV) Psalm 138:7.

"You deliver me in a day of trouble," (NAS) Psalm 41:1.

"You are my present help in trouble," (NAS) Psalm 46:1.

Understanding

"You give me understanding in all things," (NKJV) II Timothy 2: 7.

"Your word gives me light and understanding," (NAS) Psalm 119:130.

"You give me understanding according to Your word," Psalm 119:169.

"You understand my thought from afar," (NAS) Psalm 139:2.

Vengeance

"You are vengeance for me," (NAS) II Samuel 22: 48.

Want

"I shall not want," (NAS) Psalm 23:1.

Weakness

"In my weakness is Your strength," (NAS) II Corinthians 12:9.

"Your power is perfected in my weakness," (NAS) II Corinthians 12:9.

Weary

"You give strength to the weary," (NAS) Isaiah 40:29.

Word

"Your word revives me," (NAS) Psalm 119:25.

"Your word strengthens me in my grief," (NAS) Psalm 119:28.

"Your word revives and comforts me in my affliction," (NAS) Psalm 119:50.

"Your word is a light and lamp unto my feet," (NAS) Psalm 119:105.

"Your words give me light and understanding," (NAS) Psalm 119:130.

"You give me understanding according to Your word," (NAS) Psalm 119:169.

"My hope is in Your word," (NAS) Psalm 130:5.

Work

"I am the work of Your hands," (NAS) Isaiah 64:8.

Notes

Notes

Notes